LOVE
WITHOUT
LIMITS

NICK VUJICIC

Author of the *New York Times* and international bestseller *Unstoppable*

WITH KANAE VUJICIC

LOVE
WITHOUT
LIMITS

A Remarkable Story of True Love Conquering All

WATERBROOK
PRESS

LOVE WITHOUT LIMITS
PUBLISHED BY WATERBROOK PRESS
12265 Oracle Boulevard, Suite 200
Colorado Springs, Colorado 80921

All Scripture quotations are taken or paraphrased from the New King James Version®. Copyright © 1982 by Thomas Nelson Inc. Used by permission. All rights reserved.

Details in some anecdotes and stories have been changed to protect the identities of the persons involved.

Hardcover ISBN 978-1-60142-617-8
eBook ISBN 978-1-60142-619-2

Cover design by Kristopher K. Orr; cover photography by Dean Dixon; uncredited photography (cover and interior) courtesy of the Vujicic family

Published in the United States by WaterBrook Multnomah, an imprint of the Crown Publishing Group, a division of Random House LLC, New York, a Penguin Random House Company.

WATERBROOK and its deer colophon are registered trademarks of Random House LLC.

Library of Congress Cataloging-in-Publication Data
Vujicic, Nick.
    Love without limits / Nick Vujicic with Kanae Vujicic. — First Edition.
       pages cm
    ISBN 978-1-60142-617-8 — ISBN 978-1-60142-619-2 (electronic) 1. Marriage—Religious aspects—
Christianity. 2. Love—Religious aspects—Christianity. 3. Vujicic, Nick. 4. Vujicic, Kanae. I. Vujicic, Kanae.
II. Title.
    BV835.V85 2014
    248.8'44—dc23

                                                    2014020575

Printed in the United States of America
2014—First Edition

10 9 8 7 6 5 4 3 2 1

SPECIAL SALES
Most WaterBrook Multnomah books are available at special quantity discounts when purchased in bulk by corporations, organizations, and special-interest groups. Custom imprinting or excerpting can also be done to fit special needs. For information, please e-mail SpecialMarkets@WaterBrookMultnomah.com or call 1-800-603-7051.

We thank Jesus Christ for His true,
unfailing, and never-ending love.
We dedicate this work to the glory of God and pray
that this book inspires and encourages all who are
searching for love and hope.

In loving memory of my father in-law,
Kiyoshi Miyahara,
and my uncle, Miloš Vujicic.

CONTENTS

Contents

One

Someone to Love

*W*elcome to *Love Without Limits,* a book that I hope will inspire and benefit you and many others looking for guidance on finding love and sustaining loving relationships.

This book's title springs from a couple of sources, one of which is Life Without Limbs, the nonprofit organization that supports my evangelical work around the world. The name relates to the fact that while I was born without arms or legs, my God-given purpose to inspire others has resulted not in being disabled but rather in my becoming highly enabled to live a full life without limbs.

My first book spun the *life without limbs* phrase and took it a step further. We called that book *Life Without Limits,* because in it I shared my experiences and thoughts on building a ridiculously good life no matter what challenges you face, whether they are physical, mental, or emotional.

That brings us to the origins of this book's title, *Love Without Limits.* I've often written and spoken about the insecurities that dogged me as a child and young man. Because of my lack of limbs, I feared no woman would ever love me or want to marry me. I had many doubts about my fitness as both a husband and father. Frankly, there were people close to me who had their own concerns in that regard. Some thought I would never marry or be able to support a family of my own.

For a long time, it seemed they might be right. I had the usual grade school crushes, but no long-term relationships in my teenage years. Only in my twenties did I begin to feel more confident. By the time I was twenty-seven years old, I'd had some relationships that started out strong but ended sadly. One of them, in particular, was quite serious.

When this girl broke it off because she would not move forward without her parents' blessing, I was devastated. At that point, it seemed there were very real limits to the amount of love in this world, at least for me in my quest for a wife. Even though my family and closest friends were there for me, I'd become all but convinced that no woman would want to marry such an obviously imperfect man as me.

As you will learn in the pages that follow, I was flat wrong about that. So wrong, in fact, that I'm a little embarrassed to remember how despondent and self-critical I'd become after losing at love. Many people think of me as an upbeat, undefeatable person, but when it came to matters of the heart, for a while I struggled to stay positive.

I didn't give myself enough credit, for sure, but even scarier, I didn't give enough credit to God or to His gift of lasting love between two people. I don't want you to make that mistake if you've struggled as I did while waiting for God to send someone to love you. As you likely know, God brought me an incredible woman whose capacity for loving me astounds me every day. If you take nothing else away from this book, please put the following thoughts in your heart and live accordingly. They are the primary messages I want to share.

- Never give up on love if love is what you want, because God planted that desire in your heart for a purpose.
- You are worthy of love because you are the creation of a loving Father.

- There is someone who could love you and share your life.
- A successful marriage requires reciprocal and unselfish love as well as a shared, deep, and lasting commitment.
- Parenthood will test your marriage. It will also strengthen your bonds of love, but only if you develop deep empathy and unwavering support for each other by putting your family's welfare above self-interest.
- The "work" of being married is mostly about giving up our naturally self-centered ways and learning day by day to put God first, our spouses and family second, and ourselves third.
- Your marriage, your family, and your home should always be a safe, loving, caring, and comforting place—a refuge from the world and all of its challenges.

If you need further proof of the truthfulness of the previous words, look again at the book's cover photograph. There you'll see the lovely face of my wife, Kanae, who taught me that there are no limits on love.

My wife is physically beautiful, for certain, but you can't see the half of her true beauty in any photograph. Our perfect God has filled her with His perfect love, and she, in turn, loves *me,* such an imperfect man! For that reason, I know without a doubt that love has no limits.

Still, to be loved, you must feel worthy of love, and to be worthy of love, you must be willing to make sure you are deserving of this wondrous gift. Here's the thing that many people fail to grasp: To receive love, you must first give it to someone else. This means, in essence, that you must love someone so much that you will put that person's needs ahead of your own.

You must give up "me" to create "us." Once you have abandoned yourself to the love of another, you open the door to a rich and powerful relationship that elevates your life beyond anything you might have imagined.

Kanae and I are still on the journey to building our lasting relationship. In fact, we are in the very beginning stages. We have certainly had some stumbles. It turns out that I am not a perfect husband—yet! I'm a husband-under-construction. So we don't present ourselves as experts in any way. Instead, this book is meant to share our love story with you and also to offer what we have observed and learned so far, sometimes from our own mistakes and sometimes with the help and guidance of others.

Our goal is to inspire you and to prepare you for your own quest to find lasting and unlimited love with one who fulfills you and wants to share a ridiculously good life with you.

Each of the chapters that follow focus on certain aspects of the search for love, the decision to give yourself up to love, the steps toward marriage, getting married, starting a family, and strengthening the bonds between you and your spouse over the years and through the challenges. The topics we explore include the following:

- preparing to love and be loved by giving up your "self" to another
- understanding that it doesn't take a perfect person to find a love that is perfect for you
- building a loving relationship on a solid foundation by first creating bonds of friendship, mutual respect, honesty, trust, and trustworthiness during the courtship or dating period
- trusting not only your heart but also God's plan for your life in determining whether someone is "the one"
- setting the right course for a marriage by making the decision and the proposal based on your desire to serve each other first, and also to embrace each other's families and friends as part of the relationship, as long as they bring you closer
- creating and carrying off a wedding day that focuses on your love for each other and the life you intend to build together, rather than on material things, status, or other distractions, so

that wonderful memories are made and a wonderful marriage is begun

- exploring the complex challenges and undeniable joys of sexual abstinence before marriage
- submitting to each other in marriage through loving attentiveness and empathy, rather than setting unreasonable or selfish expectations by demanding that your own needs and desires come first and foremost
- handling the joys and challenges of pregnancy by adjusting to changes in the woman's body, then creating lasting paternal and maternal bonds with your child from the moment the baby arrives
- strengthening your love for each other through the years as you progress from being a couple to being a family and as adjustments have to be made in finances, housing needs, and expectations
- embracing the fact that your spouse will change over the years, just as all people do, and learning to accept each other with a maturing love through many stages and transformations brought on by changing circumstances
- communicating with empathy and the desire to understand, rather than to react or to "fix" problems, so that conflicts are resolved through forgiveness and love triumphs over resentment, anger, and bitterness
- keeping love and togetherness strong by creating family rituals, traditions, and experiences, such as reading the Bible together, family trips, holiday gatherings, and family projects.
- remaining equally yoked in a marriage built upon growing in faith and purpose together through partnering in roles that complement each person's strengths and weaknesses

- establishing the family and the home as a safe, nurturing, harmonious, and fortifying sanctuary so that when challenges arise and tragedies occur, you will always have each other and your love to depend upon

THE AWESOME POWER OF LOVE WITHOUT LIMITS

The bonds of love that connect me to Kanae and the two of us to our son, Kiyoshi, seem to grow in strength every single day. Our life as a family is more wonderful than I'd ever dreamed possible. That thought has struck me many times since marrying Kanae and welcoming our baby boy into the world on February 13, 2013, exactly one year and a day after we were married.

Most recently, I was overwhelmed by their love while traveling without them in a commercial passenger jet at thirty thousand feet. I was returning home from a thirty-three-day trip, which was the last long leg of a rewarding but grueling four-month tour of twenty-six countries, most of them in Asia and South America. There are no words to describe how difficult it was to be away from my wife and Kiyoshi that long.

My schedule allowed for just a couple of brief visits in that four-month period. Usually there was barely enough time to exchange my dirty clothes for clean ones, so there wasn't much of a chance to connect with them.

On the road I spoke to many thousands, and I witnessed God working in amazing ways, but I'd also had some major challenges. The worst was a severe fever that struck in Bolivia. It left my bones aching and my poor body baking from the inside out for a week. I managed to keep my speaking engagements despite feeling like I'd been dragged across a thousand miles of dirt road in the Australian outback.

While it was a very rewarding trip, it was also a rough go. But those trials and tribulations weren't the reasons I found myself in tears on the final flight taking me back to Los Angeles. I was not just homesick. I was Kanae-sick and Kiyoshi-sick. I missed my wife and son like crazy!

The thought of once again receiving hugs and kisses from them was so overpowering I broke down sobbing. My caregiver, Gus, was seated next to me. I didn't want him to see me going all weeping, so I pulled my cap down over my face and pretended to be sleeping. I don't think I fooled him, though. I'm sure Gus just pretended not to hear me. I'm not a quiet sniffler. He knew I was suffering from family withdrawal.

Even though Kanae and I had been video chatting during the trip, it just wasn't the same as holding them and being close to them. I love the smells of Kanae's hair and Kiyoshi. I love his baby breath! While I was traveling, my son had his first baby tooth appear, and he stood without help for the first time. I had missed so much.

I vowed that I would never again be apart from my wife and son for so long. I don't want to be the evangelist who loves the Lord but misses out on family. If I neglect my own family and I gain the world, I lose. If Kanae and Kiyoshi are the only two people in this world I make happy, that's fine with me. I believe that this is a God-given priority in our family lives. I wanted to hold them, squeeze them, and never-ever leave them. (Hmm, might there be a song in this?) I did actually put together some lyrics for a song about returning home to my family. (Stay tuned for the single!) As I wrote the song lyrics, I was a mess. I couldn't even read what I'd typed into my cell phone, because my tears blurred the screen.

What's wrong with me? I wondered.

Then the answer came: *No, this is what's right with me! I have so much love in my life, I can hardly breathe without them!*

I was flying home to my wife and son—my family—and a life I'd often feared I would never experience. What a gift the love of another person is. And the love of a child is beyond priceless. I have never felt like a whole person until these two wonderful, loving people came into my life.

FINDING LOVE WITHOUT LIMITS

I've been traveling around the world since I was nineteen years old, and I had never been so, so happy to be returning home. Of course, for most of those years I was a single guy returning to an empty house. Back then it was always sort of a letdown to open the door after a long road trip and step into utter silence.

Some people are perfectly happy living alone and even thrive being on their own. I respect that, and there is nothing wrong with leading a solitary life if that is what fulfills you. But from the time I was a teenager, I yearned for companionship and a loving relationship.

When you want a loving partner in your life so badly and you don't have someone, there is an aching void. I've heard it said that there is a God-shaped hole in each of us. It's the place that God fills with His love while we follow His plans for our lives. I was complete and lacking nothing because of my relationship with Jesus, but I still desired strongly to be with someone. At times, I feared that day would never come. And I'd been looking to fill that void for many years before I finally found the love of my life.

For much of my childhood, I could not understand why God brought me into this world without limbs. When I finally realized that He had a purpose for me to serve as an inspiration to others, it gave my life new meaning.

For much of my young adulthood, I could not understand why God had not brought me a woman to love with all of my heart for the rest of my life. I grew angry and impatient when I put myself out there in relationships that ended in heartbreak. What I didn't know at the time was that my failed relationships offered lessons I needed to learn so that when I met my future wife, I would have a full appreciation and abundant gratitude for the wondrous gift her unconditional love represents. And then God brought me Kanae, and I finally realized that He had been preparing me for her all that time.

your worthiness for love, make sure you give others a chance too. What you expect to receive, you should give, right? That is where faith comes in. If you don't want others to judge you solely by your appearance, then be willing to look deeper into them as well.

Too often we don't even try to get to know people who have disabilities or seem "different" because, for some crazy reason, we put them in a box, reject them outright, or we're just afraid to reach out to them. When I speak to young school kids, I often ask them if they would like to be my friend. Most of them, of course, say, "Yes!" Then I'll say, "Well, if you are willing to accept me—a guy with no arms and no legs—as your friend, why would you not want to be friends with anyone else who is 'different' from you, whether they are a different race, a different faith, a different economic class, or have a mental or physical disability?"

The room usually falls quiet while that sinks in. I've had students and school officials tell me many times that they've noticed a difference in their school after their young people absorb that lesson. I hope so. I know what it is like to be rejected and isolated. Growing up, I was often insecure about my lack of limbs and being in a wheelchair. I was bullied, and I'm sure there were people who shunned me or thought I was weird.

I doubted myself too, but I never gave up on my quest for love. I felt normal even if I didn't look normal, and I had the same desires as everyone else. I wanted companionship. My heart ached for someone to share my life with, someone to trust, to confide in, and be close to.

Maybe I've repressed the boyhood memories or I chose to forget them altogether, but I don't ever remember anyone in the grade-school days flat-out rejecting me because I lacked arms and legs. Now, I'm sure there were those who thought that but didn't say it, or they just shunned me so I never got close enough to ask them. Most were very kind to me. A few became great friends. But I didn't have a true steady relationship until late in my teens.

Two

The Search for Love

My lack of limbs makes me unusual in a physical sense, but my desire to find love and be loved is no different than yours. And my journey to love without limits was really much like that of many other men and women.

Sometimes I think my search for love would make a great romantic comedy, but there were other times I was certain it was destined to be a tragedy. Now that Kanae and Kiyoshi are part of my life, I find myself looking back with more amusement than sadness at my history of stumbling down the love trail.

I sometimes hear a mother tell her daughter, "You may have to kiss a few frogs before you find your prince." Most of us do experience rejection and loneliness on our journey to romantic and lasting love. In that, I'm very much like everyone else. And if you are experiencing similar challenges, I hope that sharing my story of searching for love will give you strength, help you understand that you, too, are worthy of being loved, and inspire you to never give up on your dream of finding someone with whom you can give and receive unlimited love.

∽∾∽

My first crush was in the first grade. What can I say? I was a crush prodigy! Most of us take the pursuit of love and romance very seriously, and when

someone breaks our heart, it isn't at all amusing. But we also do some very funny and crazy things along the way, don't we?

I gave my seventh grade crush a teddy bear, but then I worried that our parents would get upset if they knew we liked each other, so she gave me one too and we told our parents we were doing a "teddy bear swap."

Being able to laugh at yourself is a very healthy attribute in your search for love. I recommend it. After all, it beats crying! One of my happily married friends says that he spent his bachelor years covered in bruises because of all the girls who kept him at bay with ten-foot poles, as in the phrase, "I wouldn't touch him with a ten-foot pole!"

If you've experienced rejection—and we all have—take heart in the fact that it will make you all the more joyful when you do find love, and the bad experiences will help you truly appreciate the blessings of loving acceptance.

Like most boys and young men, my early crushes were the result of magnetic attraction, those mysterious impulses that compel us to home in o certain girls. I was very specific and focused on who I liked, and I tended like the same pretty girls as all the other guys. It was a bit hypocritical of in retrospect. After all, I wanted girls to like me despite my lack of limbs I homed in on only the girls that everyone considered the prettiest and popular. I regret that now. As you get older you realize that there is m love than physical attraction. Some of the most beautiful people I know look at all like fashion models. Yet once you get to know them, their is striking.

The trouble is we often don't give people a chance if they don't fit of the perfect one for us. I think that's a mistake. We should be open to and getting to know anyone who wants to know us. If nothing els make many friends by following that philosophy. And you might prised to find someone to love.

While you are still looking and wanting and waiting for a ch

CRUSHED

Part of being a teen is that driving desire to fit in and be accepted, which required you to be cool enough to have a relationship. Who doesn't want to be cool and popular as a teen? I wanted to be one of the guys so much that for a time I avoided all my good Christian friends and pretended to be a tough guy. My way of playing tough was to curse a lot—something I had never done. It showed! I was probably the most awkward and uncomfortable curser in history. I finally gave it up because I embarrassed myself—and my parents. Fortunately, my Christian friends hadn't given up on me and welcomed me back into the fold once I cleaned up my act.

I had my awkward moments with girls too. Most of my crushes were secret ones. I liked one girl for nearly three years, but she probably didn't have a clue. We were friends at first because she had a boyfriend. When they broke up, I stepped up, put it all on the line, and asked her out on a date.

She turned me down and then went out with another guy who was a buddy of mine. On the one hand, I was happy they had each other, but seeing them together made me sad. I thought, *I'll never have a girl like her. She is too pretty for me.*

I decided to have a pity party. It was a small affair—table for one. Isn't it funny that we all go through those experiences, but whenever we're in the middle of them, it feels like we are all alone. We think that no one else has ever suffered like we are suffering. The truth is that even the pretty girls and the handsome guys and the most popular kids have their own stories of rejection, loneliness, and insecurity. I've yet to meet anyone who cruised through childhood and the teenage years without getting a pimple, suffering a breakup, or feeling snubbed. It's part of growing up and being human. And even though it's painful at the time, dealing with challenges and hurts can help us become more empathetic, understanding, and kinder to others.

To put it in simple terms, bad things can make you better if you handle them as learning experiences. Wouldn't you prefer to take something positive away from them instead of just playing the victim and being resentful?

You and I have the power to turn even the most painful experiences into sources of good. We can do that if we choose to think of them as part of God's plan to make us stronger and more trusting of His love as well as the love of others.

Losing at Love Hurts, But It Teaches Too

I don't know about you, but I learned some valuable lessons from being kicked around by love. Well, maybe it wasn't serious love so much as puppy love or a crush. As a teenager, I dreamed of getting married and having a family some-day, just like most people. When I heard a love song on the radio, I imagined myself with whatever girl I was interested in at that moment.

I had a major crush on one of the most popular girls in our ninth grade class. I asked her out and she said no. Well, what she actually said was some-thing every guy realizes is a *no* dressed up to seem nice: "I can't go out with you because I don't want to ruin our friendship."

I was annoyed as heck and hurt too. I moped around for months after-wards. I never understood how dating someone could "ruin" a friendship. To my way of thinking, if you are dating, you can become even better friends. Isn't that the whole idea? Her answer wasn't logical, but it was one people often use when they don't want to hurt the feelings of someone they aren't eager to date.

At least she didn't say she was busy washing her hair, cleaning the base-ment, or grooming the parakeet! The biggest surprise I ever received was the time I asked out a girl in college and she said, "I'm not looking for a boyfriend. I want someone to pop the question!" I knew she was serious, but that scared me a little. Some thought she was a girl just playing games like other girls.

Guys play games too, of course. The dating game is never easy, and in recent years it seems to be even more challenging. The old system of asking someone out on a date has pretty much been abandoned. Instead of going out one-on-one to get to know each other, young people meet in large groups and then pair up. It's less formal in some ways, but many feel it's more difficult to make a real connection. Of course, that also makes it easier to just blow off someone who doesn't interest you.

Like everyone, I can have my feelings hurt by rejection. But unlike most, I have a disability that always weighed upon me in addition to the "normal" insecurities of the dating years.

I can't remember any girl ever coming out and saying that she didn't want to date me because I had no arms and legs or because I was in a wheelchair, yet there is no doubt that my disabilities stopped some from wanting to know me better. I understood that in my head, though it was hard to accept in my heart. Unlike a bad haircut, zits, or being overweight, there was nothing I could do about my lack of limbs. The thought that no woman would want to get to know me or date me for that reason was always hanging over me.

We all have our flaws. Four of mine just happen to be more obvious than most. As much as I tried to be the normal guy I felt like, there was no escape from the fact that I didn't look like everyone else. Although I realized that God allowed me to be born this way for a purpose, there was still the problem of convincing girls to go out with me. They couldn't get past my disabilities, and it wasn't just my appearance. I'm sure some were put off by the fact that I needed assistance to do many of the most basic things, like eating and drinking. I understood that, but it still hurt.

Then there was the ultimate teenage symbol of coolness—driving a car, which I couldn't do either. When other guys my age were picking up their dates and driving them to the movies, restaurants, or concerts, I had to rely on my parents or friends to drive. It was just one more normal teenage thing that I could not do.

I tried not to dwell on my disabilities, but in my darkest moments, the temptation was to give up, go home, and hide under the blankets. Fortunately, those self-defeating urges didn't take hold for long periods. I'm naturally an optimistic guy, and my faith was a source of strength—as was my family.

But my parents had mixed feelings about my interest in girls. It was partly because they were protective of me, but partly due to their very conservative beliefs. In their view, the term *dating* had bad connotations, so they preferred *courting*. I tried to explain that a guy doesn't ask an Australian teenager if she'd like to be courted by him. Half of them would probably think you were inviting them to play tennis, the other half would think you'd just stepped out of the Middle Ages.

My dad in particular was wary of the whole concept of me dating. Many years later, after I was married to Kanae, he admitted that he never thought I would get married. When I was a teenager, he didn't show much enthusiasm when I mentioned girls I was interested in. I think he was afraid someone would break my heart.

It wasn't that he and my mum didn't want me to have friends. My parents wouldn't let me isolate myself when I was down. They encouraged me to instead reach out so that my classmates would get to know me better. I'd grown up not only with my sister and brother, but also with many rowdy cousins who'd accepted me and treated me as roughly and lovingly as they treated each other. With their help, I'd overcome self-doubts and become more outgoing. I wasn't naturally inclined to be a loner, so I didn't hide. I made friends at every opportunity.

By the time I reached the later years of high school, I'd broken through many of the social barriers and learned to move past my insecurities. My schoolmates even elected me president of the student body. Yet I wasn't a guy that the most popular girls would consider dating steadily.

This was a tough lesson, but I learned something from it. Eventually I realized that there were many other girls out there worth getting to know. I became more accepting and my circle of friends grew wider. I learned that the more accepting I was of others, the more others accepted me.

I'm not saying we should pretend to be attracted to people or date someone who doesn't interest us. Teens and adults alike can get caught up in looking for someone to date or marry according to social standing, outward appearance, and popularity rather than looking into a person's mind, values, and heart.

I guess one lesson we all need to learn is to not put up so many barriers and restrictions when it comes to looking for love. You must know that you are worthy of love and accept that maybe the love of your life won't exactly fit your perception of the perfect person for you. That doesn't mean you'll have to "settle" for someone, but it might mean that your true love will be someone not at all like you had imagined.

THE RISKS OF LOVE

When you dare to love, you put your heart and soul on the line. There is always the risk of being hurt. Sometimes the person you are certain is "the one" for you decides you are not "the one" for her or him. Most people fail at love at least once or twice before they find success, so you can take some consolation in that. All of those sad love songs and stories didn't just write themselves. Men and women who experience heartbreak wrote them to share their pain in what is a universal human experience.

You, too, will feel betrayed, humiliated, and hurt if your love for someone is not returned. You will grieve the loss of that relationship. You may feel that you will never get over it, but you will. And when true love comes, you will appreciate and love that person all the more. I promise you that!

❦

A broken heart is rarely fatal. Believe me, I know. My first serious relationship began when I was nineteen. I met her at a church camp in the United States, far from my home in Australia. My uncle Batta knew her parents and wanted me to meet her. She was also from a strong Christian background. We clicked immediately, like a dream come true.

We were serious in that we began as friends and moved quickly to the point where we wanted to be together all the time. Relationship experts say that bonds are often strongest among couples who begin as friends and build upon shared interests and values. We fit the bill in that regard. We had many serious and deep conversations. It was not a sexual relationship because we both believed in saving that for marriage. And, yes, we even talked about getting married one day.

I was close to her parents too. At first, her father was very friendly to me and became like a second father to me. I had come to the United States determined to focus on my career. I believed God was calling me to a worldwide ministry. At the time, my parents and our church leaders were opposed to this idea, for various reasons, which left me feeling alone and vulnerable despite my determination. Her father was a man of courage and deep faith, and he encouraged me to pursue my vision for speaking and taking my evangelism around the world. I certainly had no intention of falling for his daughter.

Before I'd arrived at the church camp, someone had teased that maybe I would find a girl in America. I'd laughed at that, claiming I didn't need any distractions. I insisted I was attending the camp to get where God wanted me to be spiritually. In fact, I had decided to forget all of my yearnings for companionship and to instead dedicate myself to global evangelism. It was a good and healthy ten-month period of not having a crush or thoughts of anyone.

Then I met this very attractive, faith-filled young woman who set my head to spinning. She was so easy to talk with, and being together was natural. I couldn't think of anything else but her. Right after I met her, I went back to my room to be alone with my thoughts.

I prayed, *No, no, no, God. I can't fall for this girl right now, please. She lives too far away, and I have too much to accomplish.* There is a saying, "Man plans and God laughs." I imagined God was laughing and saying, "That will teach you to make plans, Nick Vujicic!"

In my prayers I told God that I would not chase after this girl, but if He wanted us to get to know each other, she would come find me during the camp. As it turned out, she did find me one day and we quickly expressed our interest in each other. The cool thing was that our conversations seemed effortless. We talked for hours with no awkward silences, just easy chatter. Three weeks of bliss ensued.

After the church camp ended, we hung out at the homes of mutual friends and, before I left the United States, I visited her at her family's home. We talked on the phone or spent time together nearly every day. I thought of little else but her, and she said the same about me. I was infatuated, and she seemed to be very taken with me. When I told her that I wished I had hands to hold hers, she said that my lack of limbs "makes it even more special."

Our time together was as close to heaven on earth as I'd ever experienced. We shared our dreams and our fears. We found so many common interests and viewpoints. I bared my soul and opened my heart to her, and I wanted to be with her every minute. We seemed destined to be together forever, and the short amount of time we knew each other felt like an entire lifetime. Then one day, seemingly out of the blue, she said, "I need some space. I'm not ready for a serious relationship right now."

This was not a good sign. A friend had once told me that if a girl ever told me she needed space, I should give her at least five thousand miles and never look back. I didn't have enough frequent flyer miles to do that. Instead, I honored her request, as difficult as it was to do. I backed off. My heart ached, but I trusted God to decide whether or not we belonged together. I told myself that whichever way our relationship went, it would be God's way—not something I had forced. You can't force love.

I did mention to Him, however, that I was very much on the side of being with her. Just in case He wondered.

When this wonderful girl told me she needed space, I wasn't sure if she really wanted to break up or if her parents were influencing her. My instincts told me that her father liked me fine as a family friend but not as a suitor for his daughter. She could not easily ignore him if that was the case. She had asked me to step back for a while, so I did, knowing that you can't make someone love you if those feelings aren't in the person's heart. I felt that if God wanted us to be together He would work it out. So I surrendered to His will.

I tried to be patient, yet the more I waited for her the more I missed her. My feelings for her seemed to grow stronger and stronger the longer we were apart. So I guess the whole "absence makes the heart grow fonder" must have some merit after all. (Someone told me the country song version of this is called "How Can I Miss You When You Won't Go Away?")

I struggled to give her space, telling myself that if God moved her heart to love me, then I could always trust that we were meant to be together. Her feelings would be between her and the Lord. I was trying to be wise and a good Christian, even though I missed her so much. The three weeks that we'd spent together had been some of the best days of my life.

LOST AND LOVELORN

Are you familiar with the term *lovesickness*? I was the poster child for this particular malady. Every day that we were apart seemed like a year. I couldn't sleep because images of her haunted me. I tossed and turned and begged God to either send her back to me or erase her from my memory.

How lovesick was Nick? I was so stricken that I bought a bottle of her favorite perfume and sprayed it on my pillows so I could bury my face in them at night. Sometimes in the daytime too!

I'd never felt such a powerful and total attraction to another human being. She had seemed to love me as much as I'd loved her, which was an entirely new experience for me. I couldn't give up on that first love. My focus on her was intense. I wrote letters and songs to her but did not share them with her. We did not communicate at all for years, but I didn't even consider going out with anyone else.

After a very long four and a half years of giving her room, I had an opportunity to see her again when I spoke at a church near her home. I still had strong feelings for her. This time I prayed for God to give me the strength to just look into her eyes and feel friendship—and only friendship.

Before my speaking engagement, I went to her house for a visit. We went through pictures she'd taken on a recent mission trip. I had always admired her love of kids and her faith in Jesus. She is a very special person. The great thing was that even though I had been secretly journaling to her (but never sharing the entries with her) and writing songs to her (that she never heard), I finally could see her as a friend. It was a *huge* thing for me.

She came to my speaking engagement. Later, she told me, "Seeing you up there made me realize that I may be stopping one of the greatest blessings that God wants to give me."

I was shocked and couldn't believe it.

We talked through our feelings and decided to try again, but in secret. She believed her father, who had opposed our relationship, would come around one day if it was God's will. She gave me a note saying she'd dreamed about our future together.

I was traveling constantly, so most of our communication was long distance. We tried this for nearly a year, but her father found her phone bill one day and realized that she had racked up hundreds of dollars by taking my calls from Australia.

This time her dad made it very clear that he was not on board with our having a relationship. I respected this young woman as a sister in Christ and wished her the best. I did not want to be a divisive force in her family. My feelings of loss were heightened by the fact that I'd become close with the girl's father when we first became friends. I'd seen him as a mentor and encourager. I'd lost that relationship too. I mourned those losses for eighteen months. I don't know what I would have done without the friends and family members who graciously served as my consolers and encouragers. Many of them prayed for my aching heart, and the rest of me too, during this period. None of us can get through the hardships of life without the support of others. I know it wasn't the most enjoyable thing for my family and friends to hear me grieve over this failed relationship, but they stood by me with kindness and understanding. The most patient and giving included the ministry teams and my close friends Andie, Lee, Ally, Jackie, and my uncle Sam. Thank you all for your prayers and empathy.

I'm an avid believer in the power of prayer, but I sometimes found it hard to summon the strength in that difficult season. My friends seemed to understand that, and they stepped up. Where I was weak, they were strong. I encourage you to surround yourself with true friends and loving family. Be there for them, and they will be there for you.

Eventually, I felt that I'd grown in maturity by going through this difficult situation. Maybe I'd lost some of my naiveté. There was part of me that wanted to give up on love and just focus on my career and my faith. I guarded my heart for quite a while, burying my feelings and burrowing into my work and travels.

I waited, not always patiently, for God to bring the right person to me. I believed He would do that, but in all honesty, I struggled with loneliness and an aching heart for a long, long time. I called it "survival mode," because there were many days when I felt like the survivor of a giant shipwreck who was just drifting in the sea, hoping to find land or a rescue boat one day.

Over the next few years there were women who expressed an interest in me and women I was drawn to, but I decided that if God had someone for me, there would be no doubt or fear or insecurities when He introduced us. Once I made that decision, I felt freedom and a new confidence. I trusted my discernment and I trusted God as well.

In my speeches I often said God would give me a wife someday. One woman who heard me say that came up to me after a speech and said, "You may not be able to hold her hands, but you can hold her heart."

I liked the sound of that.

God Never Shortchanges Us

If God puts something in your heart, He will never shortchange you. He may take something away, but only because He has other plans for you. If you've had a relationship that didn't work out, you may feel cheated or hurt or like you never want to try again. That is understandable. I've been there.

Your feelings are legitimate. If you don't feel a sense of loss after a breakup, well, then, there must not have been much there, right? Losing at love is painful, but please remind yourself that if God has put the desire for love in your heart, He will come through.

You may be in a season of loneliness and heartache, but it will pass. Take this as a time to learn, to mature, to make yourself better and more worthy of love. Don't give up. Get up. Strengthen your body, mind, and spirit for the day when God brings you someone better to love.

I can't promise you will find that one person who is meant for you, but God can. Ours is not a limiting God. He will complete and restore you.

You can doubt me, but don't doubt Him.

Just look at the person God eventually brought into my heart!

Three

Perfectly Imperfect Love

*I*t seems difficult to believe that I once doubted love would find me. I often despaired that no woman would want a man without limbs, a man who could not hold her hand, wrap his arms around her, or carry their children.

All of that worrying and doubt and fear of loneliness vanished when Kanae came into my life. So much pain was washed away. My life changed forever the first time she simply returned my gaze and smiled.

Kanae always protests when I tell her how perfect she is. She is a humble person, which only makes her more perfect in my eyes. She is also wise beyond her years, and that is because she grew up under often-difficult circumstances. Her wisdom and humility were hard earned. Yet she is always joyful, loving, caring, and incredibly unselfish.

Love found me through God's grace. It will find you too, if that is what you want for your life. You may doubt that now, just as I once did, but I hope you will take heart in our story—a most unlikely love story of a Serbian Australian man born without limbs who found love with a beautiful young woman of Japanese Mexican heritage. We found each other even though we grew up more than nine thousand miles apart in vastly different cultures on entirely different continents.

By now you are familiar with my background, but to understand the grand possibilities of love without limits as reflected in our marriage, you should know Kanae's story too. So I turn you over to her, knowing that you will be in good company—the very best, in my mind!

∽◦⌇◦∼

By the time I met Nick, God made sure I was ready for him and ready for love. I knew what I wanted in a man and a marriage by then. I had dated other men. When Nick and I met, I was in a relationship that at one time I'd thought might lead to marriage. I eventually realized that my bond with this guy was not strong enough. He was a man I liked but did not truly love. I knew that because I didn't want to marry him as much as I wanted to fix him. That's not a good sign.

When God brought Nick to me, I was looking for a man who would commit fully to God, fight for my love, and put our relationship's interests above all else. More importantly, I was searching for the man God had chosen for me.

I was hoping to one day find a mature, godly man who would try to work out our disagreements instead of just letting them stew. I wanted a man who would be willing to take the first step, to apologize first, and to make me feel like the priority in his life just as he would be the priority in mine. Those thoughts had been forming for some time, and they came together a few days after I first met Nick at a small gathering in suburban Dallas where he was speaking. We will describe that day in more depth later.

We only spoke for a few minutes. He offered to give me his e-mail address. I said I'd get it from a mutual friend who I was sure had it. I was insecure about starting something before I could figure out where my relationship at that time was going. Definitely there was a spark between us. I was drawn to his handsome face, his smile, and his commitment to changing the world through the love of God. Honestly, the fact that he had no arms and legs did register with me, but only in passing. It was like noticing a man was tall or skinny or tan. Other things stood out much more. He had such strength of character, a fantastic smile, and eyes that seemed to see into my heart.

When he looked at me, I was drawn to him like no man I'd ever met.

In the months that followed, we struck up a friendship that definitely felt destined for something much deeper. Nick was traveling, so our talks were long-distance but very candid and heartfelt. We'd just met, but it seemed like we'd known each other from birth.

My only reservation was that I had not formally ended my relationship with the other man, my boyfriend for more than a year. We had once talked of marriage, but our relationship had been unraveling before I met Nick. I realized I'd been talking myself into the idea of marrying him, thinking I could make it work instead of knowing that he was the one I wanted to spend my life with. He was a good Christian and a good person; however, there were inconsistencies and incompatibilities that gnawed at me and kept me awake at night.

There was one red-flag incident in particular that really made me examine my heart, because it made me aware that he and I practiced our faith and even looked at the world in different ways.

One day my boyfriend became upset with me for giving a homeless man some money. My boyfriend called me gullible, saying the man would probably use the money to buy drugs, which was possible, but the circumstances moved me to give to him and also pray with him.

My boyfriend was a Christian, but he didn't seem to apply his faith in this situation and others. I had tried to get him to volunteer with me at a homeless shelter where I served a couple of times, but he refused. If he had come to know the homeless as I had, maybe he would not have judged them, or me, so harshly.

A week or so later, as I was getting ready for work one morning, the thought hit me that God was using my current relationship with my boyfriend, who was the wrong fit for me, to help me define the sort of man who would be right for me. I realized that I needed a man who would care for my dreams as much as I cared for his, someone who was equally committed to God, our relationship, and consequently, our marriage.

I had not shared this thought with anyone, including Nick. You may not believe this, but it is true. Later, when Nick and I were communicating more, one day as I stepped out of the shower with these thoughts on my mind, my cell phone rang. I was still wrapped in my towel when I picked up the phone and answered.

It was Nick, and out of the blue he said this: "If things progress for us, I just want you to know one thing: I would always fight for our relationship."

It was as if he'd been reading my mind long-distance.

"Why would you say that?" I asked because I had just been asking God for that exact thing.

Nick said it just came to him and that I needed to hear it.

Then I told him I'd been talking to God and thinking that I wanted a relationship in which the man thought our love was worth fighting for. Nick could not explain how he picked up on that, but I think we both felt God was at work.

After that phone call from Nick, I had no doubts at all that our coming together was part of God's plan. How else could two people from such distant places and such different backgrounds find themselves cast together, caught in each other's gaze, and feeling such a powerful connection?

There are no guarantees in life and so there are none in this book. I can't promise that your search for love will be rewarded. I do know, however, that if you give up on love, the odds are greater that you won't find it. So if love is what you want, stay open to it. Even if your heart has been broken in the past, let it heal and then don't be afraid to try again.

I know this also: if you come from a broken home, you may have doubts about trusting another person with your heart. You may question your ability to be a good spouse. You may not have had role models that helped you to see what it takes to sustain a marriage and to keep love alive.

That's okay. Don't let those doubts and fears stop you if marriage is what you want and you feel God wants it for you too. This book is one of many resources that can help you with your relationship and your marriage. If you didn't grow up with role models for a good marriage at home, you can still find them among your relatives, friends, and neighbors. It's okay to be a little scared about the institution of marriage. Those doubts and fears can help you realize that it does take effort to keep one alive.

Marriage can be hard even when you love the person you are married to. If you've ever lived with a sibling or a roommate, you know that when you spend a lot of time with another person, even someone you are very fond of, conflicts are inevitable. You won't always agree. You may do things that bother the other person, whether intentional or otherwise.

To sustain a marriage, a friendship, or any relationship requires effort. You will likely feel that you are giving more than you are getting, and the other person will likely feel the same way. You have to be willing to forgive, to put others first, and to work on your own flaws and failings.

Knowing yourself is the first step. It helps to understand the characteristics and experiences that influence your perceptions and actions. This allows for a higher level of self-awareness, a maturity that will help you handle the demands of a marriage.

The Journey to Love

Nick and I traveled a long way in actual miles to find each other, and we also covered a lot of emotional ground. In his speeches, my husband often expresses his belief that being born without limbs is not nearly as difficult as growing up in a broken home. Well, that is part of my story and part of my journey, which is not all that unusual in these times of high divorce rates. I don't claim to be unique in that regard, although my brothers and sister and I did stand out in our hometown for other reasons.

We were known as "the Japanese family" while growing up in the Mexican city of Zitácuaro, in the state of Michoacán. Our hometown is in the center of the Mexican peninsula, about one hundred miles west of Mexico City. It is a beautiful area of pine forests, mountains, and lakes, known as the wintering place for millions of monarch butterflies that migrate from the U.S. and Canada. There is a very beautiful nature preserve in Michoacán where the butterflies gather each year after their journey.

My siblings and I stood out in our community, thanks to the Asian features we inherited from our Japanese father. We definitely were the only Miyaharas in the local phone book. Our father, Kiyoshi, had come to Mexico from Japan in his job as an agricultural engineer for an international company. My Mexican mom, Esmeralda, worked as a secretary at the same company, and so did her mother, my grandmother.

There was a large contingent of Japanese employees at the company, and my mother had put together a collection of coins and stamps from Japan and other foreign countries. She also had a Japanese coin necklace. My grandmother encouraged my shy mother to ask my father about the value of some of her Japanese coins.

That conversation led to them going out to coffee. Their relationship grew slowly, in part because neither of them was fluent in the other's language. They did discover that they had a few things in common. He collected stamps too, and they both collected seashells.

My father might have tripped up a little when he told my mother that he would never marry a Mexican woman, because they usually want to have too many kids. But as it turned out, my mother had been the oldest child in her family and she had raised her siblings, so she wasn't interested in having more than two of her own children. When she told him that, my father was relieved.

(Of course they would have four children together, but God always has His own plan, doesn't He?)

There were some doubts expressed on my mother's side as well. My grand-mother once told my father that she didn't want her grandchildren to be too short. He was a bit on the short side, but apparently they worked that out.

They married and started a family. My brother Keisuke was first, followed by my sister, Yoshie, then me, and finally my brother Kenzi.

I was just five years old when my parents decided to go their own ways, so I'm afraid their marriage didn't provide much of a role model for me. We spent half of our childhood with each parent. Our friends and neighbors who did not know our mother tended to look at our father and our Asian features and refer to us as "the Japanese family." My siblings and I considered ourselves more Mexi-can than Japanese because we lived in Mexico and spoke Spanish. Actually, many of the locals couldn't distinguish one Asian nationality from another, so many classmates and even adults called us "the Chinese."

In elementary school we endured some bullying and teasing, but nothing severe. The other kids would sing a song about a little lost Chinese girl to me, but it was not a bad song. There was also a rhyme about a "dirty" Chinese girl that wasn't so nice, and some kids would recite that when I was around, which hurt my feelings at first but then later it was like, "Whatever!"

Truthfully, most of the time being the only Asian kids in our school and our town—maybe in our whole state—was pretty cool. I made a lot of friends and never really felt rejected or isolated.

Broken Family

My luck changed when the time to live with my mother came. We were excited to see her and thought we were all going on a vacation, but that wasn't the case. Our mom took us to live with her new boyfriend, and moving in with him was not a pleasant experience. It was very difficult to be away from our father and with this man we did not know well. The only joy and blessing that came out of that relationship for me was the birth of my baby brother Abraham.

We lived with Abraham's dad for several months before my oldest brother, Keisuke, began having serious problems in school, even though he'd always been a very good student. We'd always called him "a walking brain" because he is very smart. In fact, he eventually went on to medical school and is now a doctor finishing his first specialty in internal medicine. Back then he rebelled against our mother and our life with her, so he made a decision to go back to live with our father.

My sister, younger brother, and I eventually made a case to go back to him too, and we were very relieved when our mother agreed that letting us go home was the best thing for us at that time. She knew she couldn't provide on her own and give us what she thought we deserved.

Our father was not the sort of man who hugged and kissed us and said he loved us, but he showed us how he felt by the way he acted and how he cared for us every single day. In the Mexican culture, most fathers are very expressive. My friends' fathers hugged and kissed them, and I missed out on that, but over the years I realized that my father expressed his love in his own way, like any other parent does. He made us the most amazing breakfast every day. With him we always had the best meals, family trips, and traditions—like talking over tea.

Learning to Earn Our Own Way

Our father did not give us everything we wanted, of course. We had only the basics as far as clothes, shoes, and toys, but he gave us other gifts. For one thing, he taught us how to earn a living by giving us jobs and paying us allowances when we did them well.

By my teen years, our father had opened a small store and business built around his love of tropical fish, ponds, and landscaping. We sold Japanese koi fish and many other fresh and saltwater species, as well as outdoor plants, cactus, and especially orchids. My dad loved orchids, and we had hundreds of them in his greenhouse.

We all helped out. He paid us 5 percent of our sales, which we recorded and showed him on payday. We always enjoyed going with Dad to the ranch where he leased space to grow plants and keep his fish breeding tanks. We'd ride out there in the back of his pickup truck, which had a camper top with a hole in the roof that my brothers and sister and I would put our heads through. Once he drove off the main road onto the dirt path to the ranch, Dad would go nuts, driving left and right, swerving all over so we were thrown around in the back of the camper. We loved it!

Our dad had an interesting sense of humor, but he was also very strict about keeping us in line. Dad was a man of yes and no, never much in between. If it was a no, there was no changing his mind. He had his rules, and we were expected to follow them. We were not allowed to get up from the dinner table if we still had food on the plate. There was no wasting food, but he made us eat on a timer. If we started complaining and saying that we were full, we had five minutes to finish or we'd be grounded.

I gave him more trouble than my siblings, I think. I was hardheaded. Four or five times I got a spanking, and my butt was so bruised I couldn't sit. I brought it on myself by defying him. I'd sneak out of the house as a teenager to smoke cigarettes and hang out with friends, even though I knew better. With Dad, rules were rules.

We weren't allowed to go to sleepovers at other kids' houses or have them at our house, and if we were even five minutes late for curfew, there was a steep price to pay. Still, my dad showed us love in many ways. He gave us piggyback rides, and we had tickle fights and jumped on the bed.

Change of Fortune

Our ability to run the store would prove to be a lifesaver later when our father was tragically diagnosed with leukemia. After he returned to Japan for treatment, our mother came as often as she could, leaving my youngest brother Abraham and his father behind. Despite this sacrifice, we often found ourselves to be on our own. We ran the store and lived off the proceeds. Those two years were filled with challenges and sadness. I was sixteen, and it was just my little brother and me. My oldest brother was studying and living in another city, and my older sister moved to Texas to live with relatives that same year. I cooked and cleaned and, with Kenzi's help, ran Dad's business from our home.

My dad taught us so many things and did so much for us. One of the many things I admire about him was that while he was getting treatment in Japan, he called us regularly, and then as soon as he felt well enough, he traveled that long journey back to Mexico to be with us. Every time we saw him he was full of energy. He seemed to have almost supernatural strength, even though he was undergoing chemotherapy treatments. He always encouraged us and set the business back on track as best he could before he'd have to leave again for treatments in Japan. This routine went on for a very long two years until, sadly, my dad died in Japan. My brother Keisuke was by his side at the time. Unfortunately, there was no money for our mother, my other siblings, or me to go to his funeral.

My aunt and cousins in Texas, whom Yoshie had moved in with, were Christians, and while she was living with them, Yoshie began going to church and became a Christian. Our family went to church on occasion with my mother, though not after my parents divorced. Our spiritual life was undeveloped, but before our father died, he went into a coma and Yoshie was moved to write him a letter about accepting Jesus Christ as his Lord and Savior. With Keisuke reading it to him, we believe our father did respond.

Later, when I moved in with Yoshie, the family took me to church with them. Over time, I came to accept Jesus Christ into my life too. The loss of my father and absence of my mother had left me without much guidance. I had so much grief, loss, and emptiness that I couldn't resist God's love when I heard His call.

I was eighteen years old when I became a Christian, and once I surrendered to His will, my life quickly changed for the better. My mother had already become a stronger believer in Christ during my father's illness, and over time we reunited in forgiveness and love. Our relationship has grown even stronger since I became a Christian, and stronger still since my marriage to Nick and the birth of Kiyoshi.

One of the blessings of our reconciliation was the opportunity to bond with my brother Abraham. We have always embraced him as a member of our family. My mother has said that when we make mistakes in life, there is often a high price to pay, but the hurt she experienced eventually led her to a better relationship with not only her children but with Jesus Christ.

The Bible says that all things work together for good to those who love God. My mother is now active in a ministry, and she prays passionately for others in need who reach out for her help. Now that she and I have reconciled, Nick and I both have a great relationship with her. She teasingly calls him *príncipe,* which means "prince," and she enjoys his efforts to speak Spanish with an Australian accent, which is often very humorous.

Our family has never been more content in the Lord.

New Priorities

Once I became a Christian, my priorities for a relationship changed. I had dated a few guys, and up until that point, I was drawn to boys who were cute or cool without giving much thought to their character or their faith. That changed as I grew more mature as a believer myself.

After a year of being in the serious relationship I mentioned earlier, we both began to think about marriage, but he pushed for it more than I did. There were red flags for me. He was a nice guy and had many good attributes, but there were things that bothered me and made me uncertain.

He didn't like hanging out much with my aunt and cousins, whom I was close to. He was happiest when we were alone together, and that may have been under-standable at times, but you want your boyfriend or future husband to get along with all of your family. My aunt once told me that he wasn't the person God wanted me to be with. That upset me and I defended him, but in my heart I knew I was upset because she'd told me something I felt deep down too.

I thought we were in love, but I eventually realized I was just in a comfort zone. We had been dating a year, and in the Christian world you don't normally date for much longer than that. You either get married or look for someone else. We knew we didn't want to keep dating for two or three years. We talked about marriage, and I found myself thinking that it was the next step, but there wasn't much excitement in my thoughts.

I kept thinking, *I could make this work,* which isn't really what you should feel about getting married. I know that passion and romance last only a short time, but there has to be more to getting married than simply thinking it is the next step or that it could work out okay.

I felt I didn't love him as much as he loved me. My spirit was battling with doubts. I kept telling myself that no one was perfect and that people could change, but there were serious concerns. At night, when I'd try to envision myself married to him and whether it would work over the long term or not, I found I had strong doubts. I conceded that most people contemplating marriage have some doubts and concerns. You have to be realistic and understand that no one is perfect, don't you? Wouldn't it be nice if you could take a matrimony test that was as exact as a pregnancy test? Not in the same way, of course! (I'm blushing.)

There will be conflicts and misunderstandings in any relationship. The key question is how they are resolved. Sometimes you may completely understand each other's positions but still disagree. In that case, you will simply have to agree to disagree and let it go. If there is something you can't let go, and it festers, then you have a problem.

You should think hard before marrying someone if you can't forgive, overlook, accept, or deal with issues that you may have with that person. People do change—sometimes for the better, sometimes for the worse. But if people who care about you feel a person is not right for you, I suggest you at least hear them out and reconsider the long-term prospects for a marriage.

The red flags that should send you running immediately from any relationship are those that involve abuse of any kind, whether physical, emotional, or sexual. Although this was not a problem in my relationship, drug and alcohol abuse and any criminal behavior are also unacceptable. Again, people can change their ways, reform, and go on to become a great husband or wife. It's okay to give people a chance, just make them prove it before you commit to a marriage—please!

I know what it is like to have strong doubts about a relationship, and I know what it is like to be in a relationship that feels absolutely right. There is a huge difference, and in the chapters that follow, Nick and I will share our journey to love, marriage, and parenthood with you. We don't hold ourselves up to be the perfect couple in the perfect marriage, nor are we experts, by any means. Our goal is simply to share our experiences with you—so far—in our relationship and to encourage you, above all else, to never give up on love if that is what is in your heart!

Four

The Spark

*N*ick here! I have written and talked many times about my initial impressions and feelings upon meeting my future wife, so we thought it would be fun for you to hear her side of the story in this chapter, which may help you in your own search for the perfect person for you. Kanae might have wonderful things to say about me, and I wouldn't want to deny her that opportunity, right?

So here is the story from Kanae's point of view.

As I noted earlier, I first met Nick when he gave a little talk to a small group of supporters and friends in suburban Dallas. He has written and talked about our first meeting from his perspective, but I wanted to offer my own as an introduction to this chapter, which may be of help to anyone trying to figure out whether someone is "the one" for them.

Neither Nick nor I have easy answers for that question. We wish we could give you precise tools for finding the perfect match, but all we can do is share our experiences and offer some guidance and suggestions. Our main goal is to give you hope that there is someone out there for you, if the desire to get married is in your heart.

Nick and I weren't aware of it when we first met, but we were both at the stage where we wondered whether we'd ever find true love. Then, to our surprise, true love found us!

You may have similar concerns if you've had relationships that didn't work out or if you were attracted to someone who didn't feel the same way about you. I know it's not much of a consolation if your heart feels broken, but many of us go through heartbreak before finding the right person. If finding love were easy, most of us would end up marrying our first kindergarten crush. The truth is that having a loving relationship and making it last through all the years of a marriage requires emotional maturity. I think that maybe I needed to learn what I didn't want in a relationship before I really knew what I did want.

By the time I met Nick, I had grown up a lot and I'd realized that there were certain things I wanted and didn't want in the man I married. So if you have had relationships that didn't work out, it might help you to think of them as learning experiences that will help you find someone who is a better match—maybe even perfect for you!

First Impressions

There was definitely a spark and a strong attraction from the first moments I locked eyes with Nick. Honestly, I was caught by surprise. Nick tells everyone that when he was speaking that day back in 2010, he looked out into the crowd, locked eyes with me, and had to force himself to look away.

I just wish I could say the same thing, Nick!

Just kidding. Except it is true that I didn't force myself to look away. I didn't have to because he was the speaker and I was just part of the audience. I had the luxury of staying focused on him, but he couldn't do that.

We both felt something. I wasn't sure what it was. Magic in the air? Maybe! Of course Nick is such a compelling speaker that I wondered if he wasn't having the same effect on everyone in the room. He has those warm and beautiful blue eyes, and that Australian accent is not bad, either. When he speaks, you just have to pay attention, right?

I was aware that he didn't have arms and legs, of course, but as most people who've met him will tell you, Nick has such a magnetic personality that you pretty much forget all about that in the first ten minutes of listening to him. It wasn't just his appearance that drew me in. He talked about his faith and his desire to share it with people all around the world. I was drawn to his message and impressed with the depth of his commitment.

Nick said he had a heart for broken people because of his disabilities and his struggles even before he identified his own purpose. I was just amazed at this man of God who wanted to touch hearts, save souls, and make a difference in the world.

I noticed that his eyes kept coming back to me, but I wasn't sure if that was anything more than a very skilled speaker making eye contact with his audience members. Later, Nick told me that he was torn emotionally because he wanted to keep looking at me, but he was afraid people would notice. Then he was afraid that if he didn't look at me more, I might think he was ignoring me!

We laugh now at all the inner drama we experienced during his short speech. We may have seemed calm on the surface, but all of these thoughts and emotions were swirling in our heads and hearts. I was feeling something I'd never felt before. I wasn't sure what it was in the moment. I had this strong attraction to him, but I was questioning myself: *What is this I feel? Is it his eyes that are drawing me in? His passion for his work? His faith? His accent? All of the above?*

Once you hit your twenties, relationships seem to get much more complicated, don't they? I guess it's a good thing that we become more mature and we think long-term instead of just jumping into relationships, but I also wonder if people tend to be too self-protective after they've had one or two bad experiences. We second-guess ourselves and our feelings, and that can be a good thing, but it can also be too much of a good thing.

There is risk involved in love and relationships. You can be aware of that, but you shouldn't be afraid of it. Yes, you can get hurt. But what's the saying, "Nothing ventured, nothing gained"? The romantic version of that would be the line from the Tennyson poem: "'Tis better to have loved and lost than never to have loved at all."

Give Love a Chance

You can't build a wall around your heart if you hope to give it to someone someday. What you can do is listen to both your heart and your mind. But don't be so afraid of being hurt that you are unwilling to give love a chance.

As Nick and I took the first steps of getting to know each other, we were both guarded. We did this little dance—one step in, one step back, one step in, one step back—wondering whether it was safe to get closer or stay back. We were both a bit wary because of past relationships. We didn't want to hurt each other, and we wanted to guard our own hearts too. Nick had struggled with self-doubt about his worthiness as a husband, and he'd been burned once or twice after putting his heart on the line.

I'd had my own ups and downs in relationships, and I had a little baggage because my parents had divorced when I was very young. Maybe you come from a similar background. It's pretty common these days, I'm sad to say. Nick and I hope our story can help you—not because we are special but because our experiences are like those of so many people. If we can find love, we think you can too. We want to encourage you in your journey. There's no reason to give up on love and marriage just because you come from a broken family, or because you've had relationships that failed. And it's okay to be a little scared and cautious. That's understandable. It's part of your survival instincts.

You should never jump into a relationship without getting to know the person's background, beliefs, and character. I'm not suggesting that you turn on the bright lights and the lie detector, but I've had too many friends enter into relationships with people just because they were attracted to them physically—only to discover that they weren't right for them later on.

Nick and I didn't dive into a relationship immediately, and that turned out to be a good thing because we both needed to work through some issues. It took us a while to get together, not only because we were being cautious, but also because he was traveling so much.

There was also a big tangled web of confusion that complicated things after our first meeting. It now seems like something out of a romantic comedy movie plot, but at the time it wasn't funny.

After Nick first met my sister Yoshie and me at the gathering outside Dallas, Tammy, a mutual friend who is also a speaker and writer, wanted to play cupid for Nick and Yoshie since she knew I already had a boyfriend. She sent Nick a text asking, "What did you think?"

Nick assumed that Tammy was asking about me when he responded, "She is the most beautiful woman of God I've ever met in my life. She literally took my breath away!"

Tammy, who still had in mind my sister and not me, responded, "Good, she liked you too!"

Because no names were mentioned, Nick assumed Tammy was referring to me, not my sister. The would-be matchmaker then told Yoshie that Nick had said he wanted to get to know her better.

Nick even sent Tammy a poem to give to me, but she mistakenly thought it was intended for Yoshie, so she gave it to her instead! When Yoshie told me about all of this, I was confused because at our first meeting, Nick had asked for my e-mail address, saying he wanted to get to know me better. Now do you see why I felt trapped in a very complicated romantic comedy? Yoshie would later say that she wasn't attracted to Nick like I was, but she felt maybe God was trying to put them together, so she felt she should give him a chance.

I didn't want to get between Yoshie and Nick if our matchmaker friend was right. Complicating all of this was the fact that, technically, I still had a boyfriend, even though we were going through a tough time and on the verge of breaking up. Because of that, I felt I didn't have a right to say anything. So I stepped back and stayed quiet.

Eventually, things sorted themselves out anyway, but it was a bit awkward for a while. As you can imagine, the confusion over which sister Nick liked created a delicate situation and it took a while to straighten things out. Yoshie, who noticed that there were sparks between Nick and me, was very cool about it when we finally figured it all out. But I'm happy to say she found love and got married just a year or so after Nick and I did!

It's Complicated!

Who ever said love is easy? There always seem to be complications and mis-understandings as you get to know each other and settle into a relationship. Life is messy. Love is too. But sometimes you have to fight for what you want. As a Christian, I relied on God to give me strength and wisdom throughout those try-ing and confusing times. I prayed a lot and Nick did too.

Later, Nick told me that he became very frustrated. He felt sure God had brought me into his life for a purpose, but then he feared I was slipping away. He had given me his e-mail, through Tammy, but I hadn't given him mine. He kept praying and asking God why I hadn't e-mailed or contacted him after our first meeting. I hadn't contacted him because I still had a boyfriend, and I hadn't told Nick about him when we met. Then there was the confusion over whether Nick liked Yoshie or me! The situation was a little crazy.

I had many conversations with God, asking for guidance, because I had so many doubts about my boyfriend, and the feelings I had when I met Nick were beyond any I'd experienced. My boyfriend was talking marriage, but I realized we were not right for each other. I asked God for help in ending that relationship and for His guidance on whether Nick was the man for me. I felt like God had brought Nick to me at that moment in time because we were meant to be together.

But how do you know for sure? That is always the big question.

I guess it was too much to ask God to send my future husband to me on a white horse with the angels playing trumpets! Apparently, He wanted me to figure this out for myself, with His guidance. So I asked myself a few commonsense questions and gave my preliminary answers from my brain—by way of my heart.

Do you feel a spark, a connection, a strong attraction not just to his appearance but also to his personality and his character?

Yes!

Because your Christian faith is so important to you, do you feel his faith is just as important to him? Do you share the same Christian beliefs?

Yes!

Do you think this is a man who would feel welcomed and be welcomed by your family and friends?

Yes!

Is this a man you could see becoming a loving and supporting husband to you and father to your children?

Yes!

Do you see yourself being happy to be with this man anywhere life takes you?

Yes!

Is there anything about him that makes you wary, or even nervous or scared?

No!

I didn't feel entirely comfortable answering all of those questions until I broke up with my boyfriend and began dating Nick and getting to know him better. Still, my preliminary answers, even when I knew him just a little bit, were all positive.

I know you are probably wondering what impact his lack of limbs had on my thinking early on. That is a fair question. I had never dated anyone with a disability. I knew very few people who relied on a wheelchair to get around. I certainly did not know anyone else who'd been born without arms and legs.

That said, I had a hard time even associating the word *disability* with Nick, because he is so dynamic and skilled at putting people at ease by doing most things for himself. His lack of limbs wasn't something that I gave much thought to until we became more serious. Still, even when I had a better grasp of the many physical challenges Nick deals with every day, I didn't dwell on what he lacked. Instead, I was intensely drawn to him as a person, as a friend, and, yes, as someone whom I could have a relationship with and possibly love for a long, long time.

Nick is such a strong person with a powerful sense of purpose and a great spirit. He is very skilled at handling himself and his physical challenges with complete grace and no self-consciousness. That's not to say he hasn't had to deal with insecurities and self-doubt over the years, and even now. But then, so have I, and it's fair to say most people are the same way.

I didn't know much about Nick, his ministry, or the fact that he was something of a celebrity because of his videos and appearances around the world. I was working part time as a baby-sitter and taking college prerequisites to get into nursing school. After I learned more about Nick and his ministry, I watched his videos on YouTube. I realized then that Nick was kind of a big deal, and I felt that I wasn't.

My insecurities kicked in: Why would such a successful and celebrated man like this be interested in me? How could I ever talk to him when he has seen so much of the world and I have seen so little? Later Nick would tell me that he, too, was nagged by insecurities during and after our first meeting. When I didn't send him my e-mail address, he thought I'd snubbed him!

Isn't it silly the torture we put ourselves through? Wouldn't it have been terribly sad if Nick and I had just decided that we weren't worthy of each other and walked away? How often does it happen that you meet someone and sparks fly? If you are both single and not committed to another relationship, my advice is to give it a chance. Don't let insecurities and self-doubts block you from making a connection that could turn into a loving relationship.

Overconfidence isn't a good thing, but most of us could use a little more confidence during our single years. What's really funny is that while Nick and I were drawn to each other but still dancing around each other, complete strangers were putting us together as a good match!

During that first meeting in Dallas, Nick and I talked off and on in brief conversations as his friends and fans came up to greet him. At one point I was feeling like I shouldn't be taking up any of Nick's time, so I started to walk away, but he quickly called me to come back and talk to him. It was difficult because there was actually a line of people wanting to meet with him, so I just hung back and talked to Nick between his conversations with others.

Nick and I were both shocked when at least two people that day turned to me while they were talking to Nick and said, "How long have you two been together?" Seriously!

They couldn't believe it when we said we'd just met. Some of them insisted on taking pictures of us together, and I still have those photographs from our first meeting. At the time they were taken, I remember thinking, *Wow, maybe there is something going on here if other people are seeing it!*

If you have self-doubts and insecurities about someone you are attracted to, don't be afraid to ask friends you trust to give you their input, but also trust your heart. I know it's scary to put yourself out there. Believe me, I was a not-so-hot mess that day in Dallas and for several weeks after meeting Nick because I didn't know what to do.

As a Christian, I had a secret weapon. I leaned on my faith, asking God to guide me according to His will. Sometimes I think we get caught up in the romantic fantasy stories we learn from childhood and the media. You know, the whole "Prince Charming meets Cinderella" thing. We get scared if we have any uncertainty about the person or whether we're smart enough or attractive enough.

In my earlier dating days I was guilty of focusing on a guy's appearance more than his character, and that is another mistake single women and men often make. You have to be physically attracted to the person, but don't be so rigid that the other person has to look like a movie star or you won't even consider going out. I've heard girls and guys say, "I really like this person I met, even though they aren't what I'd normally consider my type." That sounds like typecasting, doesn't it?

If you feel an attraction, follow your heart, not some preconceived notion of what your future husband or wife needs to look like. I think we should feel free to have our own love story, don't you? God may want you to find love in a way that isn't in the storybooks or movie plots, so be prepared for that and don't be afraid if what you experience follows its own narrative path. You can ask God for this. He is all about love, right?

I reasoned that God went to a lot of work to put a poor girl from a remote town in Mexico in the same room in Dallas, Texas, with a globetrotting Australian evangelist who was living in California. There had to be a reason for that, didn't there?

Five

Daring to Trust the Heart

*A*fter our first meeting in April, I didn't see Kanae for three months because I was traveling. Still, I couldn't stop thinking about her. While I was on the road, I'd send poetry to her through our mutual friend. Little did I realize that our friend Tammy was mistakenly playing matchmaker with Kanae's sister, Yoshie, instead, forwarding the poems meant for Kanae to her.

This mix-up was like something out of Shakespeare. Misunderstandings and miscommunications kept piling up, one after the other, while I was on the speaking tour. All I could think about was Kanae, but I didn't hear a word from her, not even an e-mail. When she didn't respond, I thought maybe it was her reserved Japanese side. I decided that I wasn't in a rush and would just drop a seed or two and let things play out. Of course she'd never given me her e-mail address or her cell number, so I couldn't contact her. Her silence was baffling, but I refused to ask Tammy for her contact details because I didn't want to pressure her and e-mail directly. So I was happy to just wait it out after asking Tammy to forward a few messages on to her for me. It was July before another speaking engagement brought me close to her again in Dallas.

I normally stayed with my friends Mark and his wife (my matchmaker), Tammy, when I was in the area. They were friends with Kanae and her sister, because she and Yoshie sometimes baby-sat for them. It didn't escape me that

Kanae was a frequent visitor to their suburban home, so I also just happened to ask if Kanae was around. They said she was visiting, but she'd gone out on a bike ride—with her boyfriend.

Boyfriend?

Kanae had never mentioned a boyfriend. At first I thought my hostess was joking. Then she said, "But Yoshie is here and waiting to see you!"

Is she joking? A boyfriend? And why is she telling me Yoshie is waiting to see me?

Tammy's mention of Yoshie was my first hint that my matchmaking friend was making the wrong match, mistakenly thinking I was interested in Kanae's sister instead of Kanae. When I arrived at Tammy's house, it became all too clear that she was encouraging Yoshie to talk to me while they prepared a lasagna dinner.

"So, really, where is Kanae?" I asked, still hoping the mention of a boyfriend was a joke.

"Nick, she really is riding bikes with her boyfriend," Tammy said.

That's when it sank in that Tammy had assumed I was interested in Yoshie because Kanae had a boyfriend. Of course, no one had told *me* about the boyfriend until that day. I had never exactly mentioned which of the beautiful sisters I was interested in either, and Yoshie was single and closer to my age, so I could see how Tammy made the mistake.

I felt as if someone had dropped a sack of concrete on my back. It only got worse when Kanae came back to the house with the very real boyfriend. I had been looking forward to seeing her, but now I wanted to just crawl in a dark hole. He ran upstairs to wash up, so I didn't meet him right away. Kanae gave me a warm hug and seemed not to notice my cold shoulder.

I was struggling with the fact that she was in a *relationship*. "So you have a boyfriend?" I said, trying to keep the disappointment out of my voice. "How long have you been going out together?"

When she told me that they'd been dating about a year, I felt like such a dummy. It seemed that I'd totally misread Kanae at our first meeting. Apparently she was just being friendly and kind and wasn't attracted to me at all. *She had a boyfriend!*

I felt like fleeing and checking into a hotel or canceling my appearance in Dallas and booking a flight home. I was embarrassed and uncomfortable as dinner began, but Yoshie and Kanae—and even the boyfriend whom I wanted to dislike—were being so nice to me, I decided to stay and make the best of it.

I tried to coach myself into an attitude adjustment: *Get over it. She's beyond your reach. Buck it up and move on.*

I decided that my self-coaching skills needed some work.

Later that night, I retreated to a recreation room with Tammy and her kids, where I pretended to watch television while secretly wallowing in self-pity.

Kanae joined us in the recreation room after her boyfriend left. When Tammy and the kids went to bed, I was where I had long wanted to be—until just an hour or two earlier—alone with the woman of my dreams. I gave some thought to just opening my heart to her, but I decided to preserve my dignity instead. I was struggling with my despair and my feelings for her and didn't notice that she'd left her chair until she plopped down on the couch next to me and looked intently into my eyes.

This is torture! I thought. *You are so beautiful and you have no idea how I feel about you.*

"Nick, can I talk to you about something?" she said sweetly.

I tried to stick with the Mr. Cool act, but my heart was melting fast. "Sure, what's up?"

My dream girl then poured out her heart to me—about her boyfriend and her doubts about their future together. Her family also had concerns, and she had been trying to find a way to back out of the relationship gracefully for several months.

She's looking for my advice?

At that point, I should have declared a conflict of interest and begged off, but I wasn't about to do that. I loved this woman, so I just listened to her and tried to appear as wise and dispassionate as a judge in court. When she finished telling me all the reasons she wanted to break up with her boyfriend, I showed complete restraint and did not shout, "Drop him. Come to me and I will love you forever." Instead, I deferred to a higher court.

"I understand your concerns and I think they are valid," I said. "You should pray and ask God to help you make a decision."

Instead of thanking me and saying good night, Kanae lingered on the couch next to me. Maybe she heard the pounding of my heart, but for whatever reason, she began looking at me even more intently with those beautiful, warm dark eyes.

I couldn't stand it any longer. I had to find out if she had feelings for me like those I had for her. I couldn't have been so wrong, could I?

Before I could lock down my lips, I heard my voice say, "I have a question for you: What comes to your mind when I say two words: 'Bell...Tower'?" I was referring to the romantic place we first met, a landmark tower and community gathering place in McKinney, a northern suburb of Dallas. I was meeting there with a small group of friends and supporters arranged by Dr. Raymund King, who introduced me to Tammy, who brought both Yoshie and Kanae to my talk.

"Our eyes," she said. "You looked at me, and I looked at you, and I never felt anything like that before."

Whoa! I thought. *She did feel something for me!* I was excited and frustrated at this, so I asked the other question that had been nagging at me: "Why didn't you tell me that you had a boyfriend?"

"Well, you never asked," she replied.

I thought, *fair enough.* "But why didn't you e-mail me back?"

"Because Tammy told me that you liked my sister, that she literally took your breath away. So I didn't think you were interested in me."

"No, no," I replied. "There was confusion over that, I wasn't talking about her; it was you!"

"It was about me?"

"You were the one I talked to the most that day. You were the one who caught my eyes and held them during my speech, and you were the one I texted about to Tammy!"

We were both in a daze, our minds churning.

Kanae then confessed that she'd felt the same attraction to me, and that she'd been praying and fasting and asking God for guidance about how to end her relationship with the boyfriend.

"I have never felt the way I felt when you looked at me," she said.

"Are you serious?" I asked.

We both fell silent again as we tried to untangle our thoughts and feelings. She had shared her heart with me and said she was attracted to me. But she still had a boyfriend.

"What do we do?" she asked finally.

I took the high road, even though the low road was much more appealing. As much as I wanted her to break up with her boyfriend, I didn't want to be the one who pried them apart. It also was important to never hurt her relationship with her sister. It was complicated.

"We kill it. We can't do anything," I said. "We've got to let this go and give it back to God. I've done complicated before, but this is way too complicated for me. You have a boyfriend, and your sister thinks that I like her."

She was startled by that suggestion. In truth, so was I. *What was I thinking?* My self-protective instincts kicked in. I was so attracted to this girl. I had to protect myself if she decided to stick with the boyfriend.

"You'd better go now," I said.

I wanted to add, "Because if you stay, I will want to kiss you!"

I was torn between panic and joy. She had feelings for me, but she still wasn't available to me, and she might never be. My fear of being hurt and my desire to do the right thing won out. I put my feelings for her in cold storage.

"Give me a hug and we'll say good night," I said. "We need to pray for God's help. No matter what these feelings are, we need to ask God to take them away."

We agreed to pray for God's guidance, giving it up to Him.

It seemed like God had brought us together, but circumstances were keeping us apart. We said good-bye that night feeling gloomy and confused.

The next morning before I left, Tammy and Kanae and I talked through the entire misunderstanding about which sister I was interested in. Tammy apologized for her mistake and we accepted her apology.

Kanae and I agreed to say good-bye, and I decided that it would be a long time before I would see them again. I was upset, frustrated, helpless, and leaving with a heart that felt emptied.

～⊃⊂～

I had a six-week speaking tour lined up. I thought about Kanae the entire time on the road, but I tried to forget it all and leave it all behind. I was just so frustrated. I could not understand why God allowed me to feel what seemed to be strong reciprocated love, yet an obstacle made it impossible—and the obstacle involved several layers. I didn't want to talk to Kanae. I didn't want to see her or Tammy for a very long time. I prayed for Kanae and her boyfriend and asked God to help me just heal and come back to my senses again.

Mark and Tammy knew I would be coming back to Texas and offered their garage remote for future visits so I could always stay in their home. I had been going from state to state, hotel room to hotel room, and arrived back in Dallas for another speaking engagement at the end of my tour. Before meeting Mark and Tammy, I normally stayed with other friends, including my jeweler friends Bill and Leslie Noble, or with another friend Mike Moore. This time I planned on calling Mike but learned he was out of town.

I was so tired that I convinced my two work colleagues to drive an hour to Mark and Tammy's house because we had the remote for their garage door. Tammy had said she wouldn't be there, and I was not going to stay in another hotel room if I could stay at a friend's house. The last time Kanae and I had seen each other, we had exchanged cell phone numbers out of respect. So as we drove from the airport, my first text to her was, "Are you at Tammy's house?"

I was totally expecting a "No, we are out of town" response.

"Yes, why?" she texted back.

I couldn't believe it. I chuckled out loud and stared to the heavens. "Good one, God," I said. He knew I wasn't planning on seeing her, but He also knew I wanted a bed in a home and not in a hotel. *He put this together,* I thought. I smiled at His humor and did not automatically assume anything. I just thought, *Well…we'll see.*

I texted back, "I'm coming in ten minutes. Is Tammy home?"

"What? You're joking." Kanae replied.

"No, I'm not."

"Mark and the kids are home, Tammy comes in a few days."

So I got Mark's number and texted him, asking if we could come over, and he said, "Of course."

I seriously couldn't believe it. We pulled up, my caregiver put me on a high kitchen stool, and the boys went to put the bags upstairs. All of a sudden Kanae came into the kitchen. I leaned over the counter and, making a face, feeling awkward, said, "Surprise!"

She laughed and smiled, and all the feelings I'd been trying to repress came surging forth, making me feel light in the head. The chemistry was still there, no doubt about it. It had grown stronger, in fact, or at least that's how *I* felt.

I didn't know if her boyfriend was still in the picture. I wanted to hug her, but I was afraid.

Those fears disappeared when she walked up and said, "After praying all this time, God has put peace in my heart to break up with my boyfriend. I want to be with someone I can see spending the rest of my life with."

Hallelujah!

Did I say that out loud?

Maybe I did!

Kanae explained to me that the morning after I'd left Tammy's for my six-week tour, Yoshie had told her she noticed the attraction between Kanae and me. "Hey, Sis, it seems like Nick has feelings for you. If you have feelings for him, I think you should go for it." Yoshie encouraged Kanae to break up with her boyfriend and to see whether we might have the potential for a better relationship.

"I prayed for God to tell me what my feelings were for you, whether they were just a physical chemistry or emotions, or if this really was God's call for a lasting relationship," Kanae told me in Tammy's kitchen. "I didn't want to rely on my emotions. I didn't want to step forward only for that reason, so I kept praying."

When God answered her prayers, He answered mine too! The thought of being with this wonderful, caring woman for the rest of my life wiped out all memories of the many years of loneliness and heartbreak. *Thank You, God, for giving me the strength to never give up on love.* I've often been told that if you pray and stay faithful, God will never let you down and that, in fact, He will give you more than you asked for.

Sometimes He gives you exactly what you ask for. Sometimes He doesn't. I heard someone once say that God blesses you sometimes more abundantly by not giving you what you ask for. These types of desires and prayers are very close to anyone's heart and emotions. The key is you have to trust that God only has the best in store for you. If God says no to something, He says yes to something even greater. It is when you fully surrender all of your desires to His will that His perfect will is done. This has certainly been the case with my Kanae, the perfect woman for imperfect me.

Courting Confusion

Once Kanae was free, we began seeing each other and talking on the phone whenever possible. We were eager to explore the possibilities of a relationship. We felt good about the situation, because we had done the honorable thing in waiting for the issues with the boyfriend and Yoshie to be resolved. In the meantime, we had established a friendship, which is critical to building a loving relationship. We liked each other and enjoyed each other's company.

Still, we began our courtship cautiously. It had taken so much to bring us together; we both believed God was at work. But we didn't want to mess up His efforts. We wanted our dating relationship to fall in line with God's plan for us. I've heard friends talk about the "death of dating," and I've seen news accounts of this too. It seems that many of today's teens and twenty-somethings have moved away from the traditional dating pattern of previous generations.

The old-school method of dating most often involved the male asking the female out on a date—usually dinner and a movie, miniature golf, bowling, a sporting event, or some other social activity. The more modern take on dating involves groups of males and females going out together or meeting somewhere and then pairing off or "hooking up." I'm told the idea of a guy asking a girl out on a date is now considered uncool in many social circles, which I think is unfortunate.

I wonder how young people get to know each other in any depth without spending time alone together just talking and sharing their lives and interests. At the same time, it is healthy to hang out in groups while getting to know each other. I think Kanae and I found a good balance of doing both while juggling our dates together despite busy schedules.

Of course, Kanae and I didn't exactly have an old-school courtship.

There were usually many miles between us, because I was on speaking tours or home in California, so most of our early conversations were on the telephone or on Skype, the Internet conferencing service. We talked and talked and talked, sharing our stories, thoughts, and feelings.

It didn't take long for us to discover that there was an issue between us, something neither of us had expected: we didn't speak the same language!

Let me correct that: we spoke the same language, but we pronounced many words differently. It wasn't exactly a Tower of Babel level of confounding communications but more like a Serbian Australian, Japanese Mexican tag-team wrestling match with the English language.

We didn't have great difficulty understanding each other in person, but when we spoke on the phone there were serious challenges. English was Kanae's third language. She'd grown up speaking mostly Spanish, but her father had also taught her a little Japanese. People who meet her are sometimes thrown off by the fact that she has Asian features but speaks English with a Spanish accent. I find it quite charming, but in the early days of our courtship, I sometimes got lost in her translations!

Kanae says she likes my Australian accent, but in those early days of dating, our phone conversations often left her baffled. My voice tends to wear out when I'm on a speaking tour, and my early morning and late night voice can sound like a car driving down a gravel road. So those were factors in our miscommunications too.

She often asked me to repeat things I said. I'd say certain words again and again. I could tell she still wasn't getting it, because she'd try to change the subject. She was embarrassed because she couldn't understand me.

"Kanae, you don't ever have to be shy about asking me to repeat myself," I'd tell her. "I'm Australian, and they say English is a second language for us too!"

Ours was a two-way miscommunication much of the time. She has a good vocabulary of bad pronunciations in the English language. For example, when she says the word *touch,* her version rhymes with *roach.* So when she'd tell me to "Stay in *toach,*" I thought it was the cutest thing ever!

It took me the longest time to figure out that when Kanae said she liked my "moos-tetch," she was referring to the fuzzy thing under my nose. But what I really loved was that instead of saying something was "more expensive," she'd said it was "expen*sier.*"

Still, I didn't want to correct her because I thought her language mash-ups were so cute. Then one day I finally gave her the correct pronunciation of something and she became upset because I'd never told her before!

"Why didn't you tell me the first time I said it wrong?" she asked.

"Because once I figured out what you were saying, I loved your version!" I replied.

Kanae made the valid point that she wasn't the only one who tortured the English language now and then. I am a repeat offender in the crime of verb abuse. I tense up over tenses and tend to say things like "Mom and Dad is coming to dinner."

In my defense, my father often does the same thing. *Your honor, I plead heredity.*

My father and his parents, my grandparents, always spoke Serbian when they were together, and if you start mixing Serbian grammar with English grammar, it's like a two-language pileup. Every now and then, Kanae would explode in laughter when I'd slip up and let loose with a disaster such as, "I'm more smarter than I used to be."

Strange as it may seem, our co-mangling of the English language helped bring us closer as a couple. We laughed and laughed at each other's mispronunciations and grammatical disasters. Even though we were born on different continents, we shared the experience of adapting to a new country and its language and customs.

The two of us also understood what it was like to be different. As a child, Kanae stood out in school and in her town because of her Asian features and Japanese name. My lack of limbs set me apart, obviously, but I'd also grown up in a family of Serbian immigrants to Australia. My father and mother spoke only English to us because, when they first came to Australia, they were bullied and even beat up by locals, even though Australia is known for its huge immigrant population.

Kanae and I had both been put down at times for being "foreigners," so we never put each other down. Instead we laughed and felt closer because of that shared experience.

SPARKS TO FLAMES

After the initial struggle of just trying to clear the deck of confusion and entanglements, and even though there was often a great distance between us, Kanae and I had a wonderful courtship.

The courting or dating period should be the time when you learn more about each other. We are all made up of many layers based on our experiences. As someone with such evident physical disabilities, I obviously have insecurities that go beyond any trouble I have with the English language. In hours of conversation, I came to understand that Kanae had her own insecurities that sprang from being the "China girl" in her Mexican community, about her parents' divorce, and having few resources growing up.

Insecurities can make it difficult to bond into a loving relationship, or they can become sources for bonding. How does that work? Kanae and I shared certain insecurities, and so we understood each other on a deeper level. A relationship suffers when one person's actions and words trigger insecurities and heighten anxiety and stress. If, instead, you understand and ease your partner's insecurities and fears, your relationship will grow stronger.

I quickly realized that Kanae was so tuned into the feelings of those around her. Her empathy levels were off the charts. I have had many years of practice in putting others at ease about my lack of limbs. I make jokes and demonstrate how I can do most things for myself, but I still have my insecurities. She instinctively understood the things that I was sensitive about.

It was even more amazing to me how she stepped into our relationship and adapted to my physical disabilities with such grace and ease. She acted as if it was the most natural thing for her boyfriend to be in a wheelchair and unable to do things that others take for granted. People think I'm joking when I say that Kanae scratches my back before I know there is an itch, but it's true!

The more I got to know her and her background, the better I understood Kanae and who she is. Many of her qualities are a result of taking on adult responsibilities at a very young age because of her parents' divorce and then her father's illness. She became the rock of strength for her younger brother Kenzi. She is a super nurturer.

While I was insecure about my lack of limbs and whether she could love me as I am, Kanae would eventually tell me that she was more focused on her own feelings of insecurity. She was more worried about the fact that I had been traveling the world as a speaker and evangelist while she was still in school and trying to figure out exactly what she wanted to do with her life. Because I'd seen so much more of the world already, she wondered if it might be hard for her to catch up.

Kanae summed it up in this way: "You are a speaker and preacher who has traveled the world, and I haven't even started my career yet." I told her that I looked forward to having her travel with me and sharing my life and ministry experiences. I wanted her to be with me as much as possible. I felt God would direct our paths and that someday she could resume her efforts to become a nurse.

There was another hurdle for Kanae to overcome. My family and friends are very protective of me. In my single days, those closest to me were always very watchful about the women I talked about or took out to dinner. Whenever I talked to my father about girls I was interested in or showed him their photograph, he would express negative opinions about them. I'd get angry because he'd usually say these girls weren't right for me or they didn't love me enough.

I'd ask him how he knew, and he'd say, "I just know."

Looking back, I have to admit that he was always right. It's also interesting that when I first showed him a photograph of Kanae, he had nothing negative to say at all!

By the time I met Kanae, I was fairly well known thanks to all of the speaking I'd done and, especially, thanks to the many views my videos had received on YouTube and other Internet sites. Because of that public exposure, my parents were concerned about women being drawn to me for the wrong reasons. They didn't think they were bad people, but there were women who wanted to "take care" of me or come to my rescue or, in some cases, serve God by marrying me.

I didn't want a woman with that frame of mind. I wanted a woman who loved me. Isn't that what every man wants? I felt Kanae could love me just as I wanted to be loved, but frankly, I'd been wrong before. I'd been hurt more than once because I had misread someone's motives, had misjudged someone's feelings for me, or hadn't expected her family would intervene out of concern that being married to me would be too difficult. So I'm no expert. I've made plenty of mistakes in the love department.

My parents were very interested to meet Kanae, of course, and I knew they would be cautious in accepting her. But I also knew that the goodness in her heart is so obvious she would win them over quickly, and she did. One friend told me that in the first five minutes of speaking to her, he thought, *This is a wonderful woman for Nick.*

I felt the same way. In fact, falling in love with Kanae was the easiest thing I've ever done in my life. Once the path was clear, there were few arguments or misunderstandings or feelings hurt or insecurities triggered. We became instant friends and confidantes. There was a physical attraction, certainly, and we snuggled, but we were both determined to abstain from sex until we were married. I'll devote an entire chapter to this issue later in the book. Sex can be such a powerful factor in a relationship that by taking it out of the equation, you are able to focus on other aspects, like communication, shared interests, and building a strong foundation of friendship.

You will make your own choices. We can only share our experience, and we hope you make God-honoring choices. Kanae and I found so many ways to spend time together as we were building the foundation for our love. After only a short time, I wanted her to know that I was all in. I didn't want to be her friend or even just her boyfriend; I wanted to love her and be loved by her. I'd told her that I would always fight for her love. This was a big step for me. I had to let go of my fear of being hurt and rejected.

THE MEASURE OF LOVE

Putting yourself out there after you've been burned a couple of times is difficult. There were times when I'd convince myself that I was better off without a girlfriend or wife. I tried to wall off my heart. I had to overcome my fear of rejection, tear down the walls, and give love a chance again. The Bible says that perfect love casts out fear. Most interpret that passage as referring to God's love for us, though I think it can apply to the love of another person too.

Is it possible to have a perfect love between two people? If so, what is perfect love? The Bible offers a definition of perfect love between two people, one that seems to be widely accepted. It is presented in 1 Corinthians 13:4–7: "Love suffers long *and* is kind; love does not envy; love does not parade itself, is not puffed up; does not behave rudely, does not seek its own, is not provoked, thinks no evil; does not rejoice in iniquity, but rejoices in the truth; bears all things, believes all things, hopes all things, endures all things."

These verses are particularly dear to Kanae and me because our friend Garry Phelps read them at our wedding in a very touching moment. Garry is an inspiration to many people. He tells everyone he meets that his particular type of Down syndrome is a blessing, because "You always love everyone and never ever hurt anyone."

Garry's love is a love without limits, don't you think? We can learn from his courageous example as someone who embraces life and offers genuine love and concern to all.

Whether you are Christian or not, the definition of love provided in 1 Corinthians 13 is a good one, I think. And it's not just one of those pie-in-the-sky concepts. This one can be applied in real life. When you are dating someone and wondering if it's the real thing or if it's a relationship worth exploring, try road testing it against that passage. Ask yourself these questions:

- Are we patient with each other?
- Are we kind to each other?
- Do we envy each other or are we glad and grateful for the blessings in each other's lives?

- Do we feel like we have to boast and display pride to each other, or do we each feel accepted and respected?
- Are we rude to each other or considerate?
- Do we manipulate each other to get what we want? Do we feel manipulated by the other person?
- Have there been flashes of anger between us? Does either of us have to worry about setting off the other person?
- Do either of us hold grudges or harbor resentments against the other, or do we easily forgive and forget when there is a disagreement or mistake made?
- Do we have the same moral beliefs and the same clarity on what is right and wrong?
- Has either of us lied to the other? Are we both honest, or is there a tendency to stretch the truth or color it?
- Do we feel protective of each other? safe with each other? Would we stand up for each other if there were a challenge or threat from someone else?
- Do we trust each other without qualification? with our safety? with our money? with our loved ones? with our most cherished possessions?
- When we think about our future together, do we feel hopeful or concerned? Are we optimistic and excited, or do we have reservations about what the future might hold?
- Are we willing to fight through life's challenges together so that our relationship perseveres?
- Are we equally dependent on God for all the things we know we can't do on our own or even for each other?

I suggest that you take the time to review these questions and write down your answers to them if you are in a relationship or just starting one. They are not trivial questions. They can help you evaluate whether your love fits the definition that is most commonly accepted as true and attainable. Practically speaking, all relationships go through rocky times, and every day won't be full of sunshine and lollipops. Challenges will arise. So it's all the more important to take a measure of your relationship during the dating or courtship period so you know whether it is built on love or something less substantial.

You might want to keep these questions and go over them at least once a year to reassess your relationship. I say that because a relationship changes. People change. Circumstances change. If you truly love each other, you can make adjustments as your relationship matures and encounters hardships. What should not change is your level of commitment to each other and your desire to be the best partner you can possibly be.

Six

The Gift (Wrap) of Love

*I*n the early days and months of dating someone you really like, you probably won't be inclined to analyze the relationship. You'll just want to simply enjoy the early glow of love. Eventually, though, you begin to entertain thoughts of the next stage and whether this person is "the one." You might call this the "Is this the real thing?" stage, in which the relationship grows deeper, or does the opposite. In this case, of course, my feelings for Kanae grew stronger by the second. Every moment I spent with her was a revelation. She was so refreshing, so kind and loving and beautiful that all I wanted to do was stare into her eyes and spend every moment with her.

Yes, I was infatuated, or as they say in the Disney movie *Bambi*, I was "twitterpated!" Kanae and I treasure our memories of our dating days, especially all of the laughter and warmth. We both have a very silly sense of humor, which is a good thing, because silliness might be a problem if one of you is silly and the other is serious.

Fortunately, we both felt free to let loose and act as nutty as we wanted around each other. We had some epic tickling episodes. Who needs hands for tickling when you have beard stubble on your chin? And there are probably police reports with complaints from other drivers about loud music and awful singing coming from our car as we belted out Bon Jovi songs while rolling down the highway.

We love being outside, so we had a lot of picnic dates by lakes or in the mountains or on the beach. Once we went to the Ventura Pier even though it was a cold day for California. We wrapped a blanket around us and talked and talked until we both fell asleep for an hour or so, like a couple of beach bums. We loved it!

We were still in that romantic period—we had twinkly eyes and laughed at everything the other person said. I'm not sure, but I think lovebirds landed on our shoulders and butterflies orbited around our heads. We enjoyed that magical time, but we quickly realized that eventually we would move into a more mature relationship that went beyond infatuation and romance and into a deeper commitment.

My uncle Batta is a very committed Christian and a great supporter and mentor to me. He is also an extremely passionate and expressive person. He does everything with great exuberance. Batta is known especially for his long and heartfelt prayers and blessings. He can go on for hours because his faith is so deep. He is also known for his hugs. When Uncle Batta hugs you, he hugs every bone in your body—sometimes you can hear them groaning and cracking. I've had people tell me they thought they were going to pass out from lack of air while being hugged by him. You get the picture; Uncle Batta doesn't do anything halfway.

One of the things he emphasized to me when I was dating was that it wasn't enough for me to love someone. He said I needed someone who loved me in the same way at the same level. He called this "reciprocated love," because it originated from heaven as God's gift. This type of love is truly love without limits.

Uncle Batta made a good point. I think he recognized that I was obsessed with the idea of being in love, but in my younger years I wasn't looking for the right type of love. He said if your feelings about each other aren't at the same level, there will be an imbalance in the relationship. Ideally, the man and woman in the relationship each put the other person's interests ahead of their own. I know that may sound like a fairy-tale romance to some, and it may not be possible to do that every day in every way, but in general, I think it's possible for a man and wife to want the best for each other and even to sacrifice their own individual needs and desires for the benefit of their spouse. Christians believe that God created marriage when he created Adam and Eve as a couple. His idea was that they would love each other just as God loves us. The Bible reflects this in the scripture that says, "Husband, love your wives, just as Christ also loved the church and gave Himself for her" (Ephesians 5:25).

Uncle Batta may have feared that I had a tendency to let my heart take me places where I shouldn't go. I so strongly desired to have a relationship and love someone that maybe I wasn't expecting anyone to love me back with the same devotion and intensity. True love is reciprocal in that both people want the best for each other. They want to make each other feel happy and secure in the relationship. They don't worry about who gets more or gives more. There is no keeping score. They simply want to be with each other as much as they possibly can, for as long as they possibly can.

"What you need, Nick, is someone to say she loves you, that she felt a calling to love you, and that she would always love you," said Uncle Batta.

As the father of seven children, including five daughters, my uncle has counseled a lot of young people about relationships, love, and marriage. I sympathize with the guys who were interested in courting his daughters. Uncle Batta is known for having private meetings with them to quiz them on their intentions. It may not be as bad as a police interrogation, but it's definitely a high-pressure, in-depth, heart-searching situation for the guy. Uncle Batta shared with me the questions he asks each of his prospective sons-in-law, and I think they are good questions for any Christian couple to ask themselves when contemplating a serious relationship.

1. Do you love the Lord with all your heart, mind, soul, and strength?
2. Do you love this person, and does this person have reciprocal love for you?
3. Is this person the one you want to parent your children?
4. Can you imagine your life without this person?
5. Do you have any major concerns to discuss or things you want changed before marrying this person?
6. Do you promise to treat this person respectfully and cause no harm to him or her?

MATTERS OF FAITH

The first question springs from Uncle Batta's strong Christian beliefs, which he has imparted to his children: *Do you love the Lord with all your heart, mind, soul, and strength?* It's a valid question for him to ask, because he believes in the Christian principle of the man and woman in a marriage being "equally yoked," meaning that they share the same religious beliefs and depth of commitment to their faith.

Marriages are full of challenges, and Uncle Batta believes that being equally yoked in faith gives couples an advantage in dealing with those challenges. If they are of different faiths or one is a believer and the other isn't, they may not have those same advantages.

My dad believes the same things as Uncle Batta. He once said that generally men marry women thinking they will never change and women marry men hoping they will one day change. The truth seems to be more the opposite—most men never change and rarely do women stay the same! I believe God put us together so that we would build each other up and benefit from loving each other.

The struggle is to become one as a couple and to remain equally yoked so that we are strong together. Saying "I do" at the altar is one thing, but "becoming one" is a much more challenging process, as we will explore in chapter ten. Thankfully, where we are weak, God will strengthen us with His grace and wisdom.

My parents taught me that the honeymoon period comes and goes, but to continue to grow in a marriage, you obviously must share more than a physical attraction. In fact, I was taught that you must be willing to sacrifice your own desires and wants in order to serve your spouse. To do that, you need the wisdom and strength of God. That is why Uncle Batta asks his potential sons-in-law if they believe in God. He knows they will need that sort of faith to get through the challenges of marriage and life. Christian couples who are strong in faith and equally yoked generally understand that what they want is secondary to what God wants, and that what God wants for them is even better than what they want for themselves.

When we first began courting, Kanae told me that she felt I was much more experienced in matters of Christian faith than her because I'd grown up in a Christian family, while she had only accepted Jesus Christ as her Savior six years earlier. I told her that sometimes those who convert to Christianity when they are older are the strongest of all Christians because they made the decision and committed to Christ all on their own. Those of us who grew up in a Christian home can sometimes tend to just go along and say we are Christians because our parents brought us up in the faith. We may not be as fully engaged as those who meet Christ outside their family.

The more I got to know Kanae and saw how she lived and the way she treated other people, I had no doubt that we were equally yoked. In fact, I pray that my heart can be as pure and as compassionate as hers and that I will grow in faith through her example and influence.

Reciprocal Love

The second question Uncle Batta asks during courtship is this: *Do you love this person, and does this person have reciprocal love for you?*

This question is intended to measure whether the young man is truly in love and fully committed. Uncle Batta understands that some young men get caught up in a courtship because of physical attraction and don't put much thought into where the relationship is going. I've known guys who've been swept up in a romance and then one day find themselves married and wondering, *Is this really the person I want to spend the rest of my life with?*

The question goes right to the heart. It would seem obvious that the answer is yes, but if that were always the answer, there wouldn't be so many divorces. Every person contemplating marriage should take time to seriously ask whether this is a relationship built on reciprocal love or something less, such as infatuation, physical attraction, or mere friendship.

Partners in Parenthood

Question number three is Uncle Batta's early wake-up call for every young man who may not be thinking enough about the future and raising a family: *Is this person the one you want to parent your children?* He wants his daughter's suitors to give thought to what it will be like not just to marry and enjoy companionship with his daughters but also to raise children with them. One of the compelling things I learned about Kanae as we got to know each other better was that she had strong maternal instincts. Because of her parents' divorce and her father's death, she had taken on a lot of responsibility at a young age for her younger brother. Kanae has a very caring nature, and I knew she would be a great parent to our children one day.

In It for Life

The fourth question Uncle Batta asks his daughter's suitors is, *Can you imagine your life without this person?* This one goes even deeper in exploring the commitment and depth of the relationship. You have to be fully committed to someone to marry them, and this question tests to see if that level of commitment exists.

You certainly wouldn't want to marry someone who wasn't the most significant person in your life, would you? I hope not. From the moment I met Kanae, I couldn't imagine my life without her. I wanted to be with her every second of every day.

When there were twists and turns in our early days of courting and it looked like our relationship might never develop beyond friendship, I found it hard to breathe. Even though I'd been attracted to other women and felt there were some I even loved, I had never felt that way before. It was more than a physical attraction; it was like she was meant to be a part of me and my life, and so I understand exactly what Uncle Batta is looking for when he asks that of his daughters' suitors.

No Doubts

Uncle Batta's fifth question addresses the issue of unconditional love: *Do you have any major concerns to discuss or things you want changed before marrying this person?*

If someone enters into a marriage thinking that he or she will love the person only under certain conditions, such as "only if he buys us a million-dollar house" or "only if he agrees not to watch football on Sunday afternoon," there may well be challenges ahead. If you or your intended spouse have conditions for each other or each other's family, it would be wise to discuss them long before you commit to marriage. Remember that the marriage vows say "for better *or* for worse." You have to be prepared to take the good with the bad, or at least with the not so good. You are marrying an individual with unique tastes, desires, and interests. This is not your clone.

Do No Harm

And finally, number six on Uncle Batta's list of questions—*Do you promise to treat this person respectfully and cause no harm to him or her?*—also seems like an obvious yes, but again, what the in-laws consider proper treatment may be different than how it is defined by either the bride or groom.

Sadly, some people grow up in homes where domestic violence is part of life. Those individuals, whether male or female, often have difficulty breaking the cycle, even though they know it is wrong in every way to strike a spouse in anger. You should never enter into a marriage with someone who has harmed you in the past unless you are positive it will not happen again. And I do mean positive.

Marriage and parenthood can be very stressful, but violence should never be an option, and respect for each other should be maintained even when you have disagreements and misunderstandings.

A Complementary Couple Versus a Competing Couple

Kanae and I sometimes went out with other couples—friends and their dates or spouses or business associates—and it was always interesting to see how other relationships worked or didn't work. Most of them had been together longer than we had, so their relationship had moved beyond the sparkly eyes and butterflies phase. You don't want to be judgmental in these situations, but we saw these couples behave either in ways we wanted to emulate or, less often, in ways we wanted to avoid.

Some of the men and women complemented and completed each other. We could see how they made the other person feel better and want to be better because of their love and affection. Then we saw other men and women who seemed to be at war! They picked away at each other like miners with axes. It was awful. In our dates with other couples, we observed men treat their girl-friends and wives with great respect, understanding, and kindness. We also saw couples bicker and complain, and act as though they were in competition or a power struggle, which was not a behavior that I wanted to fall into with Kanae. I tried to learn from each of these experiences.

I grew up in a Serbian family, and the tradition was for the male to serve as the dominant partner in a relationship. In that culture, the man makes the decisions and they are rarely questioned. That happened to be the model I was raised around, but Kanae and I have been blessed to know a handful of great couples who provided us with a different model, in which the men shared the decision-making process with the women and often put her needs and desires ahead of their own.

I am drawn to the idea of the man and woman serving each other's interests rather than one trying to dominate and dictate to the other. Kanae taught me a great deal about that approach to love during our courtship. Actually, there was one simple thing she did that totally captured my heart and convinced me yet again that she was the woman for me.

It was my birthday, and Kanae gave me a beautiful, cool-lookin' black jacket that was very lightweight and soft, because she knows I can get overheated eas-ily. I loved the jacket, but honestly, I loved the package it came in even more.

I'd never told her—or anyone else—that receiving gifts on my birthday or Christmas had always been a little bittersweet for me. I don't expect most peo-ple to understand this, but it bothered me that on every birthday or Christmas morning, I had to ask someone to open my presents for me.

It was just awkward, especially at Christmas when my parents or my brother or sister had to stop opening their own gifts to help me with mine. I'd always felt a little sad that I couldn't unwrap and open my own gifts. So you can imagine my gratitude and awe when Kanae, who knows my heart better than anyone in the world, came up with a gift package that I could open for myself.

I'll let my amazing, perceptive, empathetic, and loving wife tell you how she did this.

It really was just a matter of getting Nick this jacket and then thinking about how I could wrap it for him so he could open it himself. He'd never said anything to me about wanting that. I just knew that he enjoyed doing things for himself, so I thought it would be nice for him to have the joy of unwrapping his own gift.

It quickly hit me that I could get a big box, remove the top, and cut free each corner with scissors so it would collapse easily. Then I pulled the sides up, put the jacket inside, and wrapped the box in ribbon so that when Nick pulled on the ribbon with his teeth or toes, the box would fall open to reveal his present inside.

It worked perfectly on his birthday, and he was so excited when it happened just the way I planned. He looked at me with such love. I knew he would like the gift, but there was a special gleam in his eyes. I thought there must be something more going on.

Then Nick told me about never being able to open his presents before this. He shared the bittersweet feelings of having to ask someone else to unwrap his gifts, and then I understood. It meant so much more to him than I'd imagined!

When Kanae explained to me how I could open her birthday gift, my appreciation and gratitude for her soared off the charts. Then, when I pulled on the ribbon and her little invention worked perfectly, I felt an overwhelming surge of love for this woman. How incredible is it that she was so sensitive to my feelings that she came up with this perfect package for me? No one had ever thought of that. No one else had ever sensed that being able to open my own present would be a gift in itself.

I knew I loved Kanae before this happened, but in that moment, for the first time, I understood the depth of her love for me. I knew that God had put me through my previous failed relationships so that I would understand and be grateful for the great gift—this enchanting and wonderful woman!

Seven

The Proposal: Setting a Course for a Loving Marriage

*I*f you are planning to make a marriage proposal, please be sure not to tell anyone—and I do mean anyone—until *after* the proposal that you bought the engagement ring. I let it slip to a few folks, and we had a couple of close calls, but I still managed to surprise Kanae.

Let's just say that I thought my carefully crafted, highly ingenious (if I do say so myself) marriage proposal could withstand any dramatic curveball thrown. I wanted it done in a way that I could do it all by myself, and the one thing Kanae always requested about this one day to come was that she just wanted and needed it done in way and time she'd never see coming.

In the end, love—and a cream puff—conquered all!

Planning and Preparing for Your Proposal

Before I share with you the wild story of my marriage proposal to Kanae, please allow me to first caution you about the trend toward outrageously elaborate, expensive, and even dangerous marriage proposals.

You may have heard about some of the most notorious examples, including the guy who paid to make his proposal aboard a specially designed Boeing 727 aircraft that creates a zero-gravity experience thirty-five thousand feet in the air. Then there was the aspiring thespian who spent ten thousand dollars to hire an acting troupe that created an entire play designed around his marriage proposal. I'm not sure what the critics said about it.

Scariest of all was the Hollywood "human torch" stunt man who poured gasoline on himself, set himself on fire, then took a flaming leap off a high dive into a swimming pool, swam to the side where his girlfriend was waiting, and said, "You make me hot. I want to get the point across that I'm on fire for you. Will you marry me?"

I'm hoping he didn't get burned.

Originality and creativity are essential when creating great memories of your marriage proposal and wedding ceremony. But you don't need to spend thousands of dollars or risk permanent injury to make it memorable. You don't have to stage a Broadway show, and you don't have to risk giving your future wife a heart attack.

My advice would be to go for romance more than show business in planning your proposal, and do it with as much class as possible. You want to be able to tell your children and grandchildren the sweet story of this big moment. You don't want it to give them nightmares or drain their inheritance fund.

Think of your engagement proposal, and the wedding ceremony too, as setting the tone for your marriage and your life together. You want them to be joyful, fun, romantic, classy, and all about your love for each other. You don't want them to resemble a circus sideshow.

PREPARING FOR FULL ENGAGEMENT

One of the trickier areas of planning an engagement is timing. I've known guys who felt pressured to propose before they were ready. You certainly don't want to rush into proposing if you are not sure you love her and want to spend the rest of your life with her. Then again, you can't keep stringing along a girl, letting her think you love her and want to marry her, but not committing to her.

Be honest with yourself and with the girl. If you aren't sure you want to marry her, tell her and let her make her own decision instead of giving her false hope or misleading her.

Christian couples who abstain from sex until marriage often are ready to commit to marriage after a year or so of dating, especially if they have their schooling out of the way and they feel financially secure. Again, I caution you not to get engaged "because it seems the right thing to do" or because "the timing is right." Marriage is a long-term commitment. You should only step into that commitment if you truly love the person and want to spend your life with her.

There are several critical topics to discuss and consider when planning this big step toward marriage. All men and women entering into marriage need to face the fact that it is no longer just about you—either you as an individual or you as a couple. When you marry someone, you also marry into that person's family and that family's culture and traditions. Entering into a marriage partnership also means that you and your spouse must be accepting of each other's beliefs in matters of faith, politics, finance, and all other realms. You don't have to agree on everything, of course, but you must be willing to accept each other's beliefs. Otherwise, you can expect conflicts that may make it difficult to stay together.

Before You Propose, Talk About What Matters Most to You

When Kanae and I realized that our relationship could last a lifetime, we were excited, and we knew there were certain topics we needed to discuss in depth before moving ahead with any plans to become engaged and get married. These matters are vital, but you shouldn't feel pressured to talk about them before you are ready. Enjoy the courtship and the romantic aspects of it as long as you can. Laugh and have as much fun as possible while you get to know each other well enough to contemplate spending your lives together.

You may be strongly attracted to each other, but you really have to like each other to sustain a marriage. Being compatible with each other is probably even more important than being sexual with each other over the long term. Kanae and I talked about this a lot during our premarital counseling sessions with our minister. We've known couples who discovered after they were married that they really didn't get along very well. One recently married girl we know called her mother one day and said, "Is it normal for my husband to make such a big deal about where I put the blender?"

That may be a relatively small issue, but if your future spouse is one to sweat the small stuff, how will it be with the really big stuff? Please make sure you are compatible for a long-term relationship. Then, if you both feel that marriage is a definite possibility, take the time to have thoughtful discussions on the following important topics. As you talk through your feelings on each of them, remember to take the long-term view. For example, your feelings about having children or the number of children you want to have may well change over time. Accept that, but make sure you want the same thing as you enter into the marriage, with the understanding that there may be an ongoing dialogue and discussion. If one of you wants a large family and the other wants no children at all, obviously you need to resolve that before becoming engaged and marrying.

Topics to Discuss Before the Marriage Proposal

Family Issues

Kanae and I are very fortunate in that we both get along well with each other's parents, siblings, and extended family. That's not to say there may not be conflicts someday, but we started out with very warm relationships all around. Family is very important to both of us.

We've both seen couples who've struggled because of divisive relationships with in-laws. Many marriages survive and even thrive despite those family conflicts, but they can cause stress in your relationship with your spouse. You would be wise to do whatever you can *before* the proposal and marriage to work out any potential issues with the in-laws. At the very least, the couple should discuss these issues with each other to get them on the table, air them out, and make a decision on how to handle them.

The long-term impact of in-law conflicts can become a tremendous burden on a marriage. I knew of a couple, for example, who struggled throughout their marriage because the wife was extremely close with her parents—to the point that she never wanted to live more than a few miles from them. There were legitimate and highly emotional reasons for this, yet you can imagine the stress this put on the marriage in a society such as ours, where working men and women often change jobs and are required by their employers to move around the country.

Many newly married couples have their first major conflicts over how much time and what holidays and vacations will be spent with each other's families and in-laws. Ask any married couple you know and they will tell you that "keeping everybody happy" can be a real challenge. You don't have to get out the calendar for the next fifty years and lock down every holiday, but you should discuss your expectations and hopes in this area of your lives. I promise you that it will be a topic of discussion throughout your marriage, so it will be helpful to establish some basic ground rules of fairness.

Spiritual Beliefs

As we've touched on previously, the Bible strongly advises that men and women who enter into marriage should be "equally yoked," meaning that they should share not only the same spiritual beliefs but also the same depth of belief. Kanae and I are grateful that we are so well matched in our Christian faith. We understand, however, that we are very fortunate.

The Bible was written in a time when most people remained in one village or town all of their lives, and married within a community that often shared one faith. In today's diverse world, men and women of vastly different faiths often travel well beyond their birthplace before finding their husband or wife.

You and your loved one could have very different spiritual beliefs and still have a strong marriage, as long as you respect and honor each other's beliefs. It is an important topic to cover before deciding to get married, because it plays into many aspects of your life. In the short term, this would include discussing who will perform the wedding service and where it will be conducted. Long-term questions related to spiritual matters include agreeing on whether birth control methods will be used, what church you will attend, and what spiritual beliefs to teach your children.

Your spiritual beliefs may change over time, but it is wise to discuss them and establish basic approaches before the marriage so there is less chance that matters of faith could become divisive later on.

Kanae and I believe that without Jesus we'd have great difficulty sustaining our marriage. We see our marriage as a bond of three—Jesus and the two of us. As the Bible says, "a threefold cord is not quickly broken." We cannot live without Him in our lives, without His love, wisdom, patience, guidance, mercy, grace, and perfect example of sacrifice. The best thing you can do for your life and for a marriage is to have a transforming, active relationship with Jesus. Our relationship with Him is the beginning and end for our hope, and it serves as the hope and power that sustains our marriage every single day.

Financial Matters

I've heard that many couples get married without ever discussing each other's financial situation, including debt, outstanding loans, and credit rating. While these topics may not be the most romantic or pleasant, I seriously advise you to share that information with each other before becoming engaged and marrying. Most financial advisors would caution you to refuse to become engaged to or marry anyone who does not offer you full disclosure and access to their vital financial information.

Is it *that* important? Well, I'm afraid it is. Money issues are at the top of the list when it comes to conflict in marriage. Marrying someone who is laden with serious debt or has a bad credit rating could impact your ability to get a job, buy a car, and rent or own a home. Now, you can deal with those issues if you get married. Many people work with their spouse to reduce debt and improve their credit. But this is information you need to share with each other before you commit to marriage.

Your future spouse deserves to know going in what the financial challenges will be for you as a couple. Most financial advisors also recommend that couples decide before marrying how they will handle finances, including who will be the primary money manager, who will balance the checkbook and pay the bills, whether both spouses want to continue working throughout the marriage, how your investments and savings will be handled, how you will prepare to pay for the education of your children, and what your financial goals will be as a couple.

I know of couples who keep entirely separate checking accounts and divvy up expenses. If you can do that amicably and it works for you, that's great, but such matters should be discussed and decided prior to becoming engaged or married because they can be very contentious. If your spouse is reluctant to discuss financial matters, you should know why. You should also come to an agreement on what your goals are for the type of lifestyle you hope to have and whether it is affordable. You may not want to open that can of worms, but believe me, better now than later!

I recently heard of a young man who was seriously contemplating asking his girlfriend of one year to marry him until she told him that her vision of a "starter home" was a million-dollar house! That definitely gave him second thoughts. While he has a good "starter" job and a bright future, he wondered if he'd ever be able to provide the lifestyle she wanted.

I've had friends and extended family members divorce their spouse over money issues, which is very sad. Sharing financial information is essential to establishing trust and trustworthiness in a marriage. If you truly are to become a couple devoted to each other's happiness and success, you will be honest and forthcoming about all matters, especially finances.

Relationship Experiences

As our courtship moved into the serious stage of considering marriage, one of the promises Kanae and I made to each other was that we would harbor no secrets that might impact our marriage one day. With that vow, we opened up our hearts and shared our experiences in past relationships, both good and bad.

We think it is important for couples considering marriage to talk honestly about their past relationships. For one thing, these discussions help each of you understand what the other is looking for and wanting to avoid in your relationship. If you don't talk about the good and the bad of past relationships, as well as the hurts and any scars that linger, then you risk these issues arising in your own marriage. For example, if the male once had a girlfriend who cheated on him with his best friend, the female will go into the marriage knowing that he is sensitive in this regard. It will also help her understand why he is no longer close to his former best friend!

Now, you should both understand that some memories from past relationships may not surface right away, or even until after you are married, so you have to give each other some slack. Few people have perfect recall in matters of the heart. Kanae and I often discussed our previous relationships, and as we shared what didn't work, we became more and more confident that what we had was truly a love without limits that would stand the test of time.

Marital Intimacy

Couples contemplating engagement should be prepared for the intimacy of sexual relations in a marriage. You should discuss your expectations together in premarital counseling and share any issues that you have with this part of your relationship. This includes fidelity, if that's a concern. You definitely want to establish that you and your future spouse will be only with each other.

Many couples benefit from premarital counseling on this topic, either with a professional counselor or a clergy member with some expertise. Christian couples sometimes have to deal with the fact that they have worked so hard to abstain from sex prior to marriage that they have difficulty accepting that sex within marriage should be joyful and guilt-free. If that is a concern, I recommend that you talk to a trusted mentor or spiritual guide before committing to marriage, so that you and your partner are in agreement.

In my travels around the world, I often encounter women and men who have suffered sexual abuse in one form or another. This is a difficult topic to discuss for most of these people because the victim often feels ashamed and somehow guilty. It's impossible for others to fully grasp the extent of the psychological, emotional, mental, and physical trauma caused by sexual abuse. Needless to say, it can leave deep scars. I would encourage anyone entering into a marriage to seek counseling for issues related to sexual abuse. If you don't deal with them before the marriage, they can arise and be a destructive force. You may feel shame and you may not want to reveal this secret to your future spouse, but if this person truly loves you, he or she should want to help you heal so that your relationship won't suffer.

You may believe that you have everything under control, or you may have buried the pain so deeply that you no longer think about it. Everyone handles trauma in their own way, but it is rare that such things stay buried forever. That is why I am suggesting that whether you plan on marrying or not, you should protect yourself and your future relationships by seeking professional guidance either with a therapist, a mental health professional, or a clergy member trained in such things. There is no shame in getting help in this situation.

Can you imagine where I might be today in my life if I had been too proud to ask for help? We all need each other and we all need God's help.

Elephant-in-the-Room Issues

The phrase "elephant in the room" refers to particularly sensitive issues and concerns, ones that you may have been hesitant to bring up before committing to marriage with your potential spouse, but nevertheless require a frank discussion. An example of a situation like this would be how a couple with different racial backgrounds will handle questions from friends, family members, and even your future children.

Political preferences can be another elephant-in-the-room issue. When you are dating and infatuated with each other, it may not seem important that her father is the Republican national chairman and your father is the Democratic national chairman. But political issues could become a challenge in your marriage unless you establish ground rules and agree to respect each other's opinions. There are couples with very different political beliefs who simply agree to disagree and have a great marriage. Just talk it through before the proposal, so you both are comfortable that this topic won't become a challenge later on.

In my case, and for many other people, a disability, chronic illness, or disease is often difficult to discuss in the early stages of a relationship, but it should be fully explored prior to committing to marriage. My mentor and friend Joni Eareckson Tada, whose ministry is focused on helping the disabled, has written and spoken in great depth and with incredible candor about the impact of her disabilities and illnesses on her marriage.

Joni became a quadriplegic as a young woman before marrying her husband, Ken Tada. Then they faced additional challenges including her chronic pain, breast cancer diagnosis, and Ken's bouts with depression. Having a disability, an illness, chronic pain, or depression can be all consuming, making it extremely difficult to be supportive and focused on your spouse. As Joni says, your love will either grow stronger or it will die when you face such challenges in your marriage. She and Ken have been through very difficult times when they became estranged and nearly gave up, but they worked on their marriage of more than thirty years and made their love stronger.

Kanae and I talked openly about my disability before we decided to commit to marriage. I told her exactly what I can do for myself and what I would need her help doing. We also discussed whether or not I would have caregivers live in our home, or nearby, and what she was comfortable in handling herself.

I didn't want her to be surprised by anything related to my disabilities once we were engaged or married. We had many long and candid discussions about our fears, concerns, and insecurities related to my lack of limbs. I worried a great deal about this. I employ trained caregivers who help me on the road and at the office. I do not want to put my wife in the same role, even if she does help me in our home and when we are alone. It's a challenge to keep the role of wife and caregiver separate, but it's one I will always do my best to overcome.

As a boy I unwittingly came to depend on my brother Aaron as a caregiver. I should not have treated him the way I did, but he is a very giving person. We have many family stories—most of which we can laugh about now—of me bossing my brother around. There is an infamous one in which I volunteered to make everyone breakfast and then began commanding Aaron to do all the required preparation and cooking!

Kanae has a giving spirit like my brother's, and I never want to take advantage of her generous heart. I want to make sure that our relationship as husband and wife, lovers and friends, stays on track. It's very true that I did not know what kind of wife I needed until I met Kanae. She is the perfect woman for me. She does not think twice about helping me, and she never seems to think of it as a chore.

When she helps me, she never does it grudgingly, but with joy. In fact, when she helps me with things like shaving or dressing, they become bonding sessions in which we talk and share our feelings. On top of that, she gives the best shave I've ever had! Have I mentioned that my wife is amazing?

We made sure to inform our parents about the importance of maintaining the distinction between wife and caregiver. We wanted them to know that we had realistic expectations.

My parents and other relatives pushed hard on these and other questions with Kanae because, as much as they loved her already, they wanted to know that she was ready for and committed to a life with me. Kanae and I have often talked about what we jokingly refer to as The Interrogation by my family members. She has an interesting take on their questions and concerns, one that makes me even more proud to be her husband.

It was an interesting day, let me tell you. The kinds of questions Nick's parents were asking came from a different perspective than I had, of course. I understand now in a bit more depth everything they went through to raise Nick and to help him become the man he is today. I often think of all the struggles and trials they faced raising him and all the things they tried in helping him achieve a quality life.

When I met Nick, I didn't care about the fact that he was missing limbs. I didn't see his weaknesses or deficiencies. I admired him and I was absolutely in love with him. I still am! So back then, when they asked me why I loved Nick and if I was aware of the challenges I'd face if I married him, I tried my best to explain my feelings and my love for him. I have to admit, though, that inside I was thinking, *Really, guys? Don't you see that Nick really isn't that disabled at all?*

Kanae's answer to that question came as no surprise to me, because she is such a loving and caring person. I knew this instinctively from the moment I met her, but then during our courtship her great capacity for empathy was displayed many times. She told my parents that even if we had five children like me, she would love them just as she loves me. Furthermore, she said that at least our children would have a great example to learn from. My parents were in awe of her response.

Naturally, my parents love me, and for them to see Kanae's genuine love for me was a beautiful experience. My wife gives love so effortlessly that I am constantly amazed she is mine to love and cherish. Early in our dating days, for example, I had an itch in the hollow of my back that I couldn't get to by rubbing against something. So I asked her a simple question, "Could you scratch my back for me, baby? I can't get to that spot. Sorry!"

Kanae took my face in her hands, looked intently into my eyes and said, "Don't ever apologize for asking me to scratch your back or help you in any way! I will always be there for you."

After that, I never had another question about how Kanae would deal with my disabilities.

Cultural Considerations

There are several other important considerations when contemplating a marriage proposal. In many cultures and families, for example, it is still very much a tradition for the aspiring groom to ask the father of the future bride for his daughter's hand in marriage before actually proposing to her.

Guys, I'm not saying you absolutely must do that—it's up to you—but if the girl's family has expectations based on their traditions and culture, you might be wise to follow that program as a show of respect. Before proposing, you might ask your girlfriend's parents, brothers, or anyone close to them what the traditions are in their family, and even how married men in the family proposed to their wives. Their responses can help you figure out what their expectations might be. It's always a good thing to keep family traditions in mind as you plan your proposal, wedding, and your married life.

In most Christian families, for example, getting the blessing of the father, the family patriarch, or her closest male relation, is considered an acknowledgment that he has been her protector and that role will be passed on to you through the marriage.

Kanae's cultural heritage is complicated by the fact that her late father was Japanese and her mother is Mexican. Those are two very different, complex cultures. I'd asked Kanae's mum for her blessing even before I started seriously courting Kanae, and later I received my parents' blessing as well. Since her father was deceased, I decided to ask her older brother, Keisuke, for Kanae's hand and his blessing. The thought of asking Keisuke made me nervous. He's a very nice guy, but their family had many struggles, and he felt responsible for his sisters and mother. We'd gotten to know each other from the time Kanae and I started dating, and I respected him a great deal.

We arranged to get together in Houston when I had an appearance scheduled there. When I told him of my love for her and asked him for her hand and permission to marry her, Keisuke said he believed I was a good man and he felt I was mature and responsible, and that I'd treat Kanae well. I knew that he had concerns about all of my travels and what that could mean for his sister, so I assured him that my goal was to take her with me on most trips, and then to cut back on travel once we started a family.

Some guys make the mistake of failing to see their relationship from the perspective of the girl's family members, who want to know that she will be loved, respected, protected, provided for, and a priority in the life of the husband. Many families have very high expectations, so it is good to know this ahead of time.

As a Christian, I tried to keep in mind while dating Kanae that she was, first of all, the daughter of God and deserved to be treated with respect. She is also her mother's daughter and the beloved sister, cousin, niece, and grand-daughter of other family members. When you marry into that circle of people who have loved and cared for your wife all of her life, you should honor them and their love for her.

Keisuke and I decided to meet up for the big talk before I gave a guest sermon at Joel Osteen's Lakewood Church, one of the largest in the country. Most of Kanae's family had come there to hear me speak, so that added to my nervousness. At least that's my excuse for the major slip-up I made.

During my speech, I was rolling along, and before I could catch myself, I said something that had long been a part of my talks before I met Kanae. I was talking about the blessings I looked forward to in life, and I said, "I don't know who my future wife will be…"

As soon as I said it, I looked out and saw Kanae, her brother Keisuke, her mother and sister, as well as other family members in the audience. I felt especially bad because I'd just asked Keisuke for his sister's hand in marriage. Now, I hadn't given Kanae the ring yet, and we hadn't announced our plans to marry, so no one else in the audience picked up on it, but I worried that Kanae and her family would think I was a bit of a heel for saying that. After the Lakewood service, I went to dinner with Kanae and her family and I apologized to them all. They laughed and said they understood it was an "oopsy," so I was very grateful and relieved that they realized I was just in the habit of saying that line.

THE PROPER PERSPECTIVE

Like most guys who'd been single for a long time, I had to take care to widen my perspective once I decided to get married. When you get serious about settling down with someone, you have to begin thinking not just about your own concerns but also those of your wife and everyone else impacted by your decisions and actions.

When planning your proposal, your priority should be to create a memory that your wife will cherish for the rest of her life. I've had friends who didn't take that into consideration. Some just tossed off their marriage proposals in casual conversation while walking in the woods or at a sporting event. I would advise against that. Their wives have reminded them about their poor planning and lack of romance ever since! Don't let that happen to you.

Plan your marriage proposal from your wife's perspective too. Think about the things you like doing together, from places you've enjoyed going to the musical interests you share. Build those shared loves and interests into your proposal, but make sure you include at least some element of surprise, because that makes for the best memories.

AND NOW BACK TO OUR ENGAGEMENT STORY

Kanae had been tipped off about my purchase of an engagement ring, so she knew a proposal was coming. I knew she knew. And we were both pretending that she didn't know. Is that complicated or what? I took it as a challenge to find a way to surprise her anyway. She might have known that I was going to propose, but she didn't know when, where, or how, right?

And so the plotting began. Did I mention I gave myself only a couple of days to set this all up? My travel schedule was a killer, so the time frame was tight, and there were a lot of pieces to line up. First of all, I had to get Kanae and her mother to travel from Dallas, where they lived, to California, where my parents and I lived. I wanted her mom to be there so she could meet my parents and be in on the celebration after I popped the question. I had to come up with an excuse for flying them out.

Since Kanae knew that my parents had just relocated from Australia to

California in order to be near me, I told her that I would fly her and her mum out to attend a housewarming party for my parents. My actual plan was to get everyone in town so I could propose on Saturday and then we could celebrate the rest of the weekend. So how could I still make the proposal a surprise? We had talked about the fact that the following Wednesday was the one-year anniversary of the first time we'd met, at the Bell Tower. So I dropped hints to Kanae about her and her mother flying to Dallas on Wednesday, and Kanae and I having a romantic date at the Bell Tower. I knew she'd probably think that I'd be proposing then, and I did nothing to discourage her from assuming that.

Very crafty, don't you think?

Kanae fell for it. She told her family that she was preparing to act surprised when I proposed to her at the Bell Tower on Wednesday. Now all I had to do was figure out how to set up the real proposal on Saturday. I'm known for pulling things out of my hat, but this would be very tricky. I didn't want to tip her off, so it had to seem like a spur-of-the-moment thing. Since we both like to go fishing, I thought about renting a boat on a lake near my home, putting a ring inside a fish, and having a scuba diver put it on her line. But that seemed risky. What if the fish came off the line and sank? And who wants to wear a ring that's been inside a fish?

THE CREAM PUFF CAPER

There was also the challenge of how to get the ring on her finger. Lacking hands, I couldn't just pull it out of my pocket and slip it on her finger. That's where the cream puffs came in. We loved the cream puffs filled with custard made by a Westlake Village bakery near my office in California. I devised a plan to put the engagement ring inside a cream puff, then I'd have Kanae feed it to me, slowly. (I heard about a guy who hid his girlfriend's engagement ring in a hamburger and she choked on it! Didn't want that to happen.) The idea was to get the ring in my mouth so I could then pretend to kiss her hand and slip it on her finger.

Next, I had to figure out a romantic setting for doing this. (Keep in mind, I'm throwing this all together on Friday morning and hoping to pull it off on Saturday.) Kanae and I enjoy sailing, so I came up with a plan to rent a sailboat in Santa Barbara. I'd have the skipper take us out into the Pacific Ocean and I'd propose there. Then he'd take us back into the marina, where our parents would be waiting to celebrate the engagement. Call it Nick's Floating Cream Puff Marriage Proposal Adventure! I just hoped it would work.

Kanae and her mother arrived from Dallas on Friday night as expected. I went to bed praying that my plan would come together. Saturday arrived as a beautiful, sunny day. I told Kanae I wanted to take her and her mum sailing. (I wanted her mum on board so she could take photos. Esmeralda was in on the plan!) She brought a camera and I instructed her to look for my signal. I said I'd wink at her when I was preparing to put the ring on Kanae's finger.

I made it all seem spontaneous and casual. Kanae had no idea what I was up to. She still was secretly thinking I would propose when we were at the Bell Tower in a few days. I had a friend pick up the tray of freshly baked cream puffs early in the morning. The one with the ring inside was chocolate covered with a special powdered sugar coating so I could tell it from the others.

We drove with Kanae and her mom—and the cream puffs stashed in a red cooler—to Santa Barbara's harbor, where we boarded the Catalina sailboat I had reserved. The skipper was waiting for us and had been instructed at my request to take us out for an hour. Then, after I'd proposed—and hopefully Kanae had accepted—we would return and pick up my mum and dad and take them out for a little celebration on the water.

What this skipper apparently had not been instructed was that I was on a secret mission, because just after we boarded he blurted out, "So we are coming back in an hour to pick up some more people, right?"

Kanae looked at me, and I shot him a look that said, "Not a word more!" Then for Kanae's benefit, I brushed it off, saying, "No, two hours out and then back. It's just us."

Fortunately, Kanae was busy getting settled on the boat and didn't ask any questions. As we left the dock, the waves were choppy and my stomach was too. I was nervous about getting the engagement ring out of the cream puff and onto Kanae's finger without dropping it or, worse, swallowing it!

There was one problem I hadn't foreseen. As we settled down in the boat with blankets and the cooler, the choppy waters were rocking the boat. The cooler was sitting on a bench, and as we picked up speed, one of the waves nearly threw it overboard—with the cream puffs and the engagement ring inside!

"Kanae, would you put the cooler under those ropes and put a towel over it?" I asked. My tone of voice betrayed my high stress level.

Kanae gave me a "What are you freaking out about?" look.

With the rough seas, I thought it was best to make my proposal sooner rather than later, so after about fifteen minutes of heading out to sea, I asked Kanae to get the cream puffs out of the cooler.

She brought the cooler over, and her mother, following the plan, went to the back of the boat, saying she wasn't feeling well and wanted to stretch her legs. When Kanae pulled the tray of cream puffs out, I told her I wanted the chocolate one.

They were big cream puffs, so she said, "Do you want the whole thing?" I nodded yes, and she put it in my mouth.

I nearly gagged. I hadn't bargained on the cream puff being such a mouthful. Kanae watched me carefully, wondering if she'd have to give me the Heimlich maneuver. I was struggling to find the engagement ring inside the cream puff while crumbs, cream, and powdered sugar spewed from my mouth.

I panicked a bit because I couldn't find the ring with my tongue, but then

I found it and calmed down. Kanae turned away from me to help herself to a cream puff as I carefully positioned the ring in my mouth. I could feel and hear the ring clattering against my teeth, but Kanae had no clue. She was looking out into the beautiful sunlit ocean.

"Hey, baby, come here. I want to kiss your hand," I said, and since I did this all the time, Kanae didn't suspect anything unusual. I looked at her left hand as I said it, so she extended that one. I bent over her hand, and as I moved to put the ring on her finger, I realized there was another challenge. I had to do it so the diamond was facing up!

You probably haven't had much experience at maneuvering a diamond engagement ring with your tongue to transfer it from your mouth to someone's finger on a rocking sailboat in the Pacific Ocean, but trust me, it's no easy feat.

Now, Kanae had grown accustomed to me kissing her hand, but when she felt me putting her finger in my mouth, she pulled back a little, so I had to be a bit more forceful to slide the ring all the way down. I didn't want it popping out into the boat or the water, did I?

At first, Kanae didn't realize what I'd done, and she looked at me strangely, like "What are you doing?" But then I looked into her eyes, and she looked at the ring on her finger and went into shock.

I couldn't exactly drop to my knees, but Kanae quickly figured out what was coming.

"Baby, I love you. Will you marry me and spend the rest of your life with me?"

"Yes, yes, yes, I'll marry you!" she said.

Honestly, I was very, very grateful that Kanae said yes, but I was probably even more grateful that I'd pulled off the surprise proposal and gotten the ring on her finger without swallowing it or spitting it into the ocean!

Okay, I was ecstatic! The seas had calmed, and the skies were a brilliant blue, and there was this beautiful young woman—my wife to be!—snuggling next to me as we headed back into the harbor. Her mother returned and took some photographs to record our engagement.

I was fairly certain life could not get any better than that moment.

Oddly enough, as we pulled into the harbor, we passed several anchored boats. There was a man with no shirt on one of them. It looked like he lived on his boat. He walked out on his deck as we passed, looked directly at Kanae and me, and shouted, "It gets better!"

Goose bumps sprang up on my arms. I felt as if God was smiling down upon us.

As we pulled into the marina, I announced to my parents, "She said yes!" We were teary-eyed as they boarded and hugged us. Our skipper then steered the sailboat out to the ocean with our merry crew on board. As we left the harbor, a large seagull joined our party. It flew just above the skipper's head, matching our speed by riding on the wind. We tossed some crackers into the air, but this bird wasn't the least bit interested in the food on our ship. It seemed as though the seagull was blessing our engagement by taking us under its wing.

"I've sailed all my life and never seen a gull do that," said the skipper.

We chose to think of our serene seagull escort as another good sign that we were on course to a wonderful life together.

Eight

Creating Wedding Day Memories

anae and I dated for a year, and then we were engaged for six months before marrying. At first that seemed like too long to wait, but the months flew by swiftly because there were so many arrangements to be made. We also needed a long lead time because we invited wedding guests from all over the world. That's what happens when your bride and groom have relatives and friends in Australia, Japan, Hong Kong, South Africa, Mexico, California, and many points in between.

We learned early in our wedding planning that it may have been *our* marriage celebration, but we were the hosts, not the guests. Your wedding day will be one of the biggest days of your life, yet it is also a huge event for those closest to you.

Our suggestion for planning and carrying out your wedding day is to begin with this thought: *This day will be about celebrating and sharing our wedding with all of those people who have loved us, cared for us, and brought us to this glorious moment in our life. Our goal for our wedding is to be a blessing to all who attend.*

This attitude will help you avoid some of the common pitfalls encountered by couples planning and staging their weddings. If you approach this wonderful day as one to be shared and celebrated with family and friends, you are less likely to become a bridezilla or a groomzilla. By taking the focus off yourself, it allows you to instead focus on making this the best day ever for your intended spouse and those closest to both of you. The goal is to relax and go with the flow, because if you worry about everything being exactly as you planned it, you'll never be able to enjoy this landmark day. And in case you were counting on having the perfect wedding, rest assured it will *not* go exactly as planned! But that's what makes it so interesting, right?

Accept that your wedding will probably have a few glitches that will give you something to laugh and tell stories about for many years to come. A calm approach to your special day will be of great value when your wildest cousin trips and falls into the wedding cake or your college roommate accidentally offends your entire family. Not that either of those things happened at *our* wedding. No, our wedding was perfect!

Well, let's put it this way: Our wedding was perfectly imperfect, just like me. (And I say that in all humility.) You don't believe me? Well, read on, and I'll tell you about our wedding song gone wrong and the terror of being pulled over by a police officer on the way to our honeymoon hotel! (No, you won't find our wedding photos on Mugshots.com.)

PRELUDE TO A WEDDING

Despite a few comic moments on our wedding day, many of our guests have told us that ours was one of the most joyful celebrations they've ever attended. Kanae and I agree, and we believe the celebratory tone was set a few months before the actual ceremony.

We were married in California, but there was a prelude to our wedding that took place in Plano, Texas. It occurred about three months after our engagement, at the home of Kanae's uncle Eduardo "Eddie" Osuna, who owns a real estate firm in the Dallas area.

I come from a very large, passionate, and fun-loving extended family. Okay,

I'll just say it: some of them, particularly my cousins, can get rowdy. This worried me a little as the wedding date approached because the members of Kanae's family whom I'd met so far were wonderful people, but they were a little more reserved than my fun-loving clan of cousins.

Kanae loves to have a good time, but she has a serene, sweet demeanor, as do her mother, sister, and brothers. So, early in our relationship, I was a little concerned—just a little—that being surrounded by my boisterous Serbian uncles, aunts, and cousins might overwhelm them.

The party at Uncle Eddie's house erased any such concerns. I learned that Serbians have nothing over Mexicans when it comes to having a good time. Uncle Eddie's party was supposed to be a small gathering of people on Kanae's mother's side. I'd already met her mum, brothers, and sister, of course. But she wanted me to meet and get to know her grandmother, Loida Medellin, and other extended family on the Mexican side.

Before we headed to Uncle Eddie's house for the "little gathering," Kanae assured me, "It will be quiet and formal. We'll probably just sit around the dinner table and talk."

As we pulled up to the front door, Kanae and I both noticed that the house was dark, but there were many faces peering out the windows at us.

"Oh my gosh, look at all the people!" said Kanae.

We parked the car, went to the front porch, and rang the bell.

The front door flew open.

The house lights flashed on.

"SURPRISE!" yelled Uncle Eddie and a chorus of about fifty people packed in behind him. Before we could close our gaping mouths, a trumpet note blasted and a twelve-piece mariachi band with violins, guitars, and horns cut loose with a welcome tune from the living room!

My first family fiesta had begun.

Kanae and I were pulled into the party and swallowed up by hugging family members dancing all around us to the mariachi music. Believe me, I've been welcomed in a lot of places, but I've never felt as welcomed as I did at Uncle Eddie's house party. I'd been in the door about two minutes when I found myself dancing with Kanae's grandmother.

The love and joy was overwhelming. Kanae's aunts, uncles, and cousins danced up one by one and introduced themselves while also serving me heaping plates of delicious Mexican food. It was awesome!

When the band took a break, they asked me to introduce myself and to talk a little about my work and how Kanae and I had met. Then Uncle Eddie and one of Kanae's closest older cousins shared their feelings for her. They said that they'd always felt protective of her family since her father's death. They admitted that they were skeptical of "the evangelist" when they first heard she was dating me. They wanted to make sure Kanae married a good man who could provide and care for her.

Uncle Eddie and a few others admitted they had some doubts about our relationship at first, but after hearing our love story, they were overwhelmed with thankfulness and joy. We all became teary-eyed. Kanae and I have had many wonderful times together, but that party was definitely a highlight and a blessing, because it set the tone for our wedding.

Meeting so many of Kanae's relatives and feeling their love for her brought home to me once again that our wedding was not just the union of two people as man and wife, it was also a celebration marking our welcome into each other's families. When I listened to Kanae's mother, sister, brothers, grandmother, aunts, uncles, and cousins sharing family stories, I was so grateful to be accepted by them.

One of the great joys in life is to be part of something bigger than your own life and experiences. When you marry, for better or worse, you do that. You become part of your spouse's family, their history, their story, and their traditions. I welcomed that opportunity because Kanae has a wonderful and honorable family. I know she felt the same way about joining my family, because they love her very much—and I am grateful for that blessing too.

WEDDING PLANNING

We knew after Uncle Eddie's fiesta that our big day would be a multicultural celebration of faith, family, and friendships. Seriously, my main fear after the party at Uncle Eddie's house was that it might be hard for our wedding to live up to that level of joy and excitement, but in the end, I think we managed to pull it off. Quite nicely, in fact.

There are many books, blogs, and websites that offer you step-by-step guidelines for planning a wedding. You should look for detailed advice from the experts and professionals. Just be aware that planning a wedding is more complicated and emotionally charged than most couples anticipate. It can be very draining, because there are so many decisions to be made—and so many people you care about involved. Feelings are easily hurt. There is also the undeniable fact that wedding costs can quickly pile up into a mountain of money. You may want the best of everything, but remember, when the honeymoon is over, the bills will be waiting at home.

Kanae and I had no expertise in planning weddings. We hope that we never have a hand in planning another one, unless it's for one of our children, or two or three of them. We can only share with you some of our observations and a few tips we picked up along the way.

Because we have such large families and so many friends scattered all over the world, our guest list quickly reached about two hundred and fifty people. We came up with a wedding budget (also known as wishful thinking), and then set out looking for a location that was within our financial means.

One of our challenges was that we decided to hold the wedding in the area near my home and office just outside Los Angeles, because so many of my relatives are there. My family is much larger than Kanae's, and she felt it would be best to have the wedding in a place they could easily reach.

We were hoping to find a scenic location near the ocean, if possible, because we both love the water. Of course we quickly realized that we were looking to plan a wedding in one of the most expensive places on earth. We spent weeks combing the region to find the right place with enough capacity for all of our guests and at a price that wouldn't force us to become panhandlers after the wedding.

One day our search took us to the Palos Verdes Peninsula, which is on the Pacific coast and known for its beautiful wedding chapels, resorts, golf courses, cliff-side mansions, great surfing beaches, and incredible scenery. Many movies and television shows are filmed in this area including portions of the *Pirates of the Caribbean* movies and *The O.C.* and *Entourage* television series.

Kanae and I checked out a wedding chapel that proved to be too small. Then we visited a gorgeous resort that offers beautiful facilities for weddings, but it was way, way, way over our budget. We were worn out and discouraged. This was about as close as we came to just eloping in Las Vegas and sending postcards to family and friends saying, "Sorry, we decided to take the quick and easy Elvis route."

By 3 p.m. I was ready to head home, but Kanae asked if we could check out the oceanfront grounds and ballroom at the Trump National Golf Club in Palos Verdes. I laughed at the thought of the two of us getting married on any property owned by Donald Trump.

I doubt if we could afford to rent The Donald's garage, I thought.

"I'd just like to see the country club. I've heard how beautiful it is," Kanae pleaded.

The drive into the Trump property is one of the most gorgeous in the world. You cruise along the manicured Palos Verdes Drive with incredible views of the Pacific Ocean and Catalina Island off to the left and cliff-side estates on the right. It's like a paradise. Kanae and I kept waiting to run into a security gate and guards telling us to go back to the real world.

We drove into the grounds and found the Grand Ballroom and Vista Terrace, the outdoor wedding area on a bluff with 180-degree views of the Pacific Ocean. Kanae picked up a brochure for their wedding services and it said, "Walk-Ins Welcome." We took that to mean walk-ins seeking information on weddings were welcome, not that we could just walk in and get married—even though that seemed like a pretty good idea right then.

Kanae and I were 99.9 percent sure that we were in way over our heads, but we were in awe of the place, so we figured we might as well check it out. We arranged to meet with their special events manager, Monika, who taught us a valuable lesson about wedding planning: if you choose the right time of year and the right day of the week, you can get a good deal, even in Trump territory.

Monika told us that our plan to have the wedding in early February was a little risky in one way and yet wise in another. The coastal weather at that time of year varies greatly, but it can be cold, windy, and rainy many days. That was the risky part. The wise part was that because February is a slow time of the year for weddings, the price for renting the ballroom and outdoor ceremony area was half of what it would be in the busier months. She then added that if we were willing to have the wedding on a Sunday, another slow day for weddings, the price would be cut in half again.

Kanae and I were astounded. The prices we'd been quoted at our last stop were two and a half times more than Donald Trump was charging for one of the most elegant places either of us had ever been.

This location was perfect! And because the ballroom was big enough for three hundred people, Monika said we could move the ceremony inside if the weather was bad. So we had a Plan B, which is always a good thing.

We were thrilled!

THE ULTIMATE WEDDING PLANNER

Once we had a location for our wedding, the other plans quickly fell into place. I said *quickly*, but not always smoothly. We were several months into the planning stages when we realized that we needed a professional. Fortunately, we found a good one, and after speaking with her for a couple of hours, Kanae realized how much we *really* needed her assistance.

She was incredibly helpful with finding a florist and a deejay within our budget. We particularly liked the fact that she understood the importance of honoring our families and their ethnic traditions. She wasn't Serbian or Mexican—in fact, she was Greek—but she got the picture immediately.

There was one element of the wedding that even the most skilled planner cannot control, especially along the Pacific coast. That cold reality hit us on the night of our rehearsal, when things ran late and we were freezing before we'd finished our run-through.

On the day of our wedding, February 12, 2012, the morning skies were a gloomy gray. The temperature hovered in the fifties for much of the morning, giving the air a chilly bite, and the gusty wind on our bluff-top ceremony site was challenging us as we erected the four-hundred-dollar wooden gazebo we bought at Lowe's because renting one was three times the price. Now we have that same gazebo in our backyard, and it's a wonderful memento of our wedding that we can look at every day and enjoy.

All morning long Kanae and I fretted and prayed over the weather, fearing the wind would pick up or the rain would come in and force us to go to Plan B. Moving the ceremony inside wasn't a terrible alternative because the ballroom was so beautiful, but it didn't have the same amazing view provided by Plan A.

The wedding ceremony was set for 3:30 p.m., which gave the sun time to climb into the sky and heat up the air a little. It was not quite sixty degrees

Fahrenheit, still overcast, and very breezy as the guests began filling the chairs facing the ocean. I had a very good view of all of this, because during a balcony photo session, my best man (brother Aaron) and the groomsmen (my cousins) all had me fall into their arms in a reclining position as they picked me up, put me over their heads, and pretended to throw me into the Pacific Ocean.

Luckily they listened when I reminded them that they wouldn't likely be fed dinner or treated to the open bar if the groom went missing at sea before the ceremony. They finally put me down, and we made our way to the grassy area on the bluff where the ceremony was to take place. With my groomsmen and best man accompanying me, I motored down in my brand-spanking-new wedding-special wheelchair designed just for this event—which I had recently acquired because my regular wheelchair had been dropped so many times by airport crews that it was no longer operational. I took my place with our pastor, Marc Schiler, under the gazebo and skies that were still covered in a gauzy gray.

I was fretting because a hotel staff member had told me that rain often moves in during the late afternoon in winter months. Then I heard this un-earthly sound, and at first I feared it was a storm approaching. Suddenly I re-membered that Kanae's sister, Yoshie, had asked to sound a couple of notes of rejoicing on a ceremonial ram's horn, or shofar, used in her church's services.

As she sounded the horn in regal tones dating back to biblical times, the overhead clouds dissipated, the wind disappeared, and the sun gently warmed everyone atop the bluff. It's true! On the video of the ceremony, you can see people slowly taking off their shawls and coats as the ushers seated our parents and the bridesmaids.

With the arrival of the sun came a radiant vision: my stunning dark-haired bride appeared in her flowing wedding dress. With her brother Keisuke escort-ing her, Kanae walked down the aisle toward me. I hardly noticed that the re-corded song playing was not Eva Cassidy singing her lovely version of Fleetwood Mac's "Songbird," which we had carefully selected for the processional. Instead, it was an entirely different song by the same name, a smooth jazz instrumental performed by Kenny G on saxophone.

I thought, *Well, that's not what we picked out, but it's okay, I guess.* I don't know what I would have done if it had been a truly *terrible* song! It really wouldn't have mattered, because at that point, the sight of Kanae gliding down the aisle had us all mesmerized.

All of our family and friends rose to their feet, and my heart soared with them. At previous weddings I'd attended, I had often commented that when I see a bride crying during a wedding ceremony, I worry about the future of the couple. So I had some explaining to do later, because I was the one fighting back the tears as Kanae walked toward me with love in her eyes.

The beautiful vision of my beaming bride coming to join me on the sunlit cliff overlooking the Pacific Ocean will be forever stored in my mind. After so many years of loneliness and heartbreak and dealing with the fear that no woman could ever love me, seeing Kanae in her gorgeous wedding dress sent my heart soaring. I've never felt such gratitude and I've never felt so much love. There was no doubt in my mind that God was at work when He put us together.

Pastor Schiler gave a wonderful talk, noting that as the Bible says, we were two becoming one, but he also noted, "You remain yourselves. You become complementary parts of a new entity.... At this moment, you can gaze into each other's eyes and it makes you happy." But then the pastor added that a good marriage grows into something more and that all aspects of love are required over a lifetime—including friendship and self-sacrifice.

"You can have a romantic relationship and a supportive relationship and a working relationship and an affectionate relationship, all at the same time," Pastor Schiler said. "The best is if you just want to make the other person happy. If you both do that, you will both be happy."

By the time the pastor asked us to say our vows, Kanae and I were battling back tears. I was more than a little nervous also, because she and I had always planned to write our own wedding vows, but we'd never gotten around to doing it. Where was my ghostwriter when I needed him?

Note to future brides and grooms: do not procrastinate when it comes to writing your vows. During our premarital counseling sessions, our counselor kept urging us to write our vows. When we still hadn't written them in time for the rehearsal, we were chastised. I was very grateful that our minister gave us some traditional, by-the-book vows, just in case we procrastinated all the way up the aisle during the wedding ceremony.

We did use those vows, but we made one small addition. Actually, it was an addition for all eternity. After the standard line about "until death do us part," we added "and be reunited in heaven."

I figured it wouldn't really be heaven if I didn't have Kanae there, right? At least as my neighbor, as we have requested. Seriously speaking, Kanae's father died when she was still young, and I wanted to reassure her that even if for some reason I was called to heaven before her, I would be there waiting for her when she arrived.

Once we said the vows, I had to once again pull off the nifty trick of putting a ring on her finger by holding it in my mouth (after my brother stealthily placed it there) and slipping it on. This time, however, there were no cream puff bits spewed in the process.

Kanae placed my wedding ring, with the words *Love prevails* engraved on the band, around my neck on a chain, and then a moment later, she raised her bridal bouquet in the air in victory, to the cheers of all. I had never been so happy in my life, and I had never felt so blessed.

A Party to Remember

The ceremony was so exciting and invigorating; Kanae and I were fired up and ready to celebrate. We had no little difficulty restraining ourselves during the mind-numbing interlude before the party. This is the period when you begin to harbor murderous thoughts toward your wedding photographer and videographer. While our friends and family merrily dashed off to start the wedding celebration, we gave ourselves up to those hired to record the day for posterity.

Be prepared for this. You paid for it. They are just doing their job, and the best of them are true artists whose work you will appreciate for the rest of your life.

Once we rejoined the party, with our eyes still blind from flashbulbs, our co-celebrants witnessed what may well have been the world's first wedding to feature a bride and groom's first dance aboard a custom electric wheelchair with the power, maneuverability, and quickness of a Porsche 911 Carrera. Loving speeches were offered by a number of guests, including my brother Aaron, my sister Michelle, my father Boris, Kanae's sister Yoshie, and Kanae's mother Esmeralda.

My brother explained that my parents had named him Aaron after the brother of Moses who, according to the Bible, was of great help to the leader of the chosen people.

"Mom and Dad saw that Nick needed help, so I got that name," Aaron said. He teased that our parents claimed "a lot of free child labor" from him as a result.

My brother also teased me about the demands I made on him growing up. He explained that he missed key parts of many movies and television shows because I was always calling him for assistance. This went on even into my late teens when I first began giving inspirational talks at schools.

Our wedding guests roared with laughter when Aaron described a typical exchange back then: "Nick would yell, 'Aaron, I need a shower,' and I'd say, 'Do it yourself!' And Nick would say, 'I can't!' and I would say, 'That's not what you say in your speeches! I believe in you, Nick! You can do it!'"

My brother brought tears to my eyes and many others at the reception when he recounted the first time I called him and told him about Kanae. "I remember the sound of joy in Nick's voice when he called, a sound like I'd never heard before, the sound of a man completely in love," he said. "I always said that Nick's wife would need to be a superwoman, and I think he has one now!"

Kanae's sister Yoshie's speech mentioned the same topic, the depth of our love for each other, and she touched the hearts of all of us in the room: "There was a season in my life when I doubted about true love, but you two changed my mind," she said. "The love you have for each other is so precious and equal and mutual and unconditional. I learned it doesn't really matter where you are, love can find you. Love also doesn't care what you do or don't do, who you are or who you aren't, because true love looks at the heart."

Yoshie was sincere in saying that she changed her mind about love after seeing ours. Just over six months after our wedding, Kanae's sister found love herself and is now married too. I seriously think Kanae and I must have started something when we fell in love because my sister Michelle was single at the wedding too. I told her then that I knew one day she would find someone. She did, just a year later.

One of the greatest blessings you can have in a marriage is the support of the parents of your spouse. I never got to meet Kiyoshi, Kanae's father, but we had a silent tribute to honor him and his love toward his children. It was a very moving moment.

The string of speeches were like waves of love, reflection, thankfulness, and joy. Remembering where we both came from and our family member's love for us brought us to streaming tears. My uncle Batta always said that the way I honor my wife is to honor her family. I endeavor to do that all my life, but that night it was so moving to see how our families honored and thanked the Lord and us as their children and siblings.

Then, when we thought we couldn't cry any more, Kanae's mother Esmer-

The day at the Bell Tower when
we both felt the sparks fly.

On the sailboat the day Nick
proposed—with the ring in
his mouth—just after he
popped the question.

Can you see Nick's
peaceful and satisfied
expression after Kanae said
yes?

Isn't she lovely? Isn't she wonderful?

Our wedding day, which ended with a memorable dance.

Carefree newlyweds honeymooning in Hawaii and—later—a skydiving adventure.
(A special thanks to Skydive Deland in Florida.)

A surprise pregnancy and the joyful arrival of baby Kiyoshi.

Enjoying new opportunities as Daddy and Mummy.

Kiyoshi chatting online with his globe-trotting daddy and looking dapper at six months.

Family love on Kiyoshi's first birthday.

alda moved us all deeply too. "If you did not believe in fairy tales, let me tell you a true one," she said. "The prince with the golden voice waited for the perfect time to meet his princess, and she met him one evening in the tower (the Bell Tower, in fact), and once she heard him, she knew he would be her prince!" She publicly thanked God that He had brought us together and how she loved my family and loved how they loved her family in return. Her sweet words were absolutely amazing. I was in awe of how beautiful and gracious she was, and how blessed I was that she was now my mum too.

My father took us to another level of emotional depth as he reflected on the day of our wedding and traced it back to the day of my birth nearly thirty years earlier: "I am excited and thankful to God for bringing us all together in this moment," he said. "God obviously had a plan I couldn't see when Nick was born. I am finding it difficult to believe that my son, Nick, is married, and not only married but to such a beautiful girl. I am speechless."

Dad continued, "It was beyond my imagination that I would ever see or come to this moment. There was a time when I experienced one of the lowest periods of my life, when all I could do was look at my baby boy and wonder what kind of life will this child have? Will he be lying in bed all his life? Will he never be able to walk or do anything?

"How wrong! How wrong was I? Sometimes our lives are like that, and we see the worst. Yet God can turn the worst into something that is beyond any dream. I am thankful to God for that."

My father's reflections and those of all who spoke that day will forever echo in my memory and guide us in our marriage. Kanae and I took every word to heart, and my dad expressed his gratitude that God provided in such an incredible way for his son. My family adores her so much.

I also felt led to ask my uncle Batta to pray. He joyfully and humbly accepted and also offered his reflections on our marriage. He noted that God's plan for Kanae and me had been playing out for a long time, because the cliffside land our reception hall was built upon had once been considered too unstable for a building—until a man whom Uncle Batta himself had mentored and trained in excavation methods succeeded in stabilizing it.

"Before he touched it, the hillside was washing out, and people said the land was worthless," Batta said. "He stabilized it and made this event possible today. It was an act of providence."

My exuberant uncle and second father then provided a beautiful wedding prayer—a brief one by his standards—along with his heartfelt reminder that we all need the Lord and that without Him we can do nothing.

Another special feature of our wedding was something you don't often see or hear. Our musical entertainment included both recorded Serbian folk music and a full mariachi band. Yes, we had a friendly battle of ethno-musicians, and I'm happy to report, Serbian-Mexican relations came away in great shape.

Taking the Cake

If you've ever helped plan a wedding or even been to a wedding in recent years, you are probably aware that there is a wedding-industrial complex out there. It consists of wedding planners, florists, decorators, dressmakers, reception halls, photographers and videographers, caterers, limo companies, musicians, deejays, jewelers, and, depending on how crazy you want to get, may even include dance instructors, jugglers, ice sculptors, and circus clowns.

According to theknot.com, the average American wedding now costs more than $29,000. In California, it's more than $38,000, and in Manhattan, more than $86,000. Some social critics think it's gotten out of hand. They blame celebrity and royal weddings for upping the ante. I don't know about that, but I do know that it really isn't about how much money you spend. It's about how much heart you put into it.

With that thought, I'd encourage you to make your wedding your own creation, rather than trying to duplicate something pulled off by a Kardashian or a member of the British royal family. Look for ways to express yourselves and your love for each other and your families. Whether that means including family photos in the decorations or having Uncle Ernie's band perform, Kanae and I think you will create even richer memories by adding your own special touches.

Our own example of that is a piece of cake. Well, actually, it was Kanae's own unique take on the traditional bride and groom figures that went atop our wedding cake. My bride is very artsy-craftsy. Like many women planning weddings, she spent a lot of time on Internet websites like Etsy and Pinterest, which are chock-full of cool creations. Kanae was looking for inspiration. Since I didn't really match the standard-issue top-of-the-cake groom figure, she decided to create one that more closely resembled me.

She purchased two wooden pegs and balls and went to work gluing them together and painting them to resemble us. As she was putting them together, Kanae decided that the balls were a bit too big to accurately portray our heads. (Well, more in her case than mine. According to my family, I've always had a big head!) So she ordered some in a slightly smaller size, started over, and painted them to look like us. I loved them. Everyone loved them. They were hilarious, and again, they helped make our wedding more personal and memorable. I also found it moving that in the midst of all the hullabaloo of planning and pulling off our wedding, Kanae took the time to lovingly craft something with her own hands.

Honestly, I think more photographs were taken of the bride and groom figures on our cake than were taken of the actual bride and groom. Okay, I'll admit it—Kanae's creation was much better looking than the guy she married, but we both have hard heads.

Wedding Night Bust

As you've probably noticed by now, Kanae and I were all about creating magical memories during our wedding. We planned some of those special moments and features, but there were more than a few that happened entirely on their own. The one that stands out wasn't exactly magical, it was more terrifying when it occurred, but we certainly have talked and laughed about it ever since.

There comes a time late in every wedding celebration when the exhausted bride and groom need to make their getaway. I don't have to tell you that it's probably not a good idea to be the last man and woman standing at your own wedding, right? Nor do you want to be the bride and groom remembered for the rest of their lives for crashing and burning in exhaustion while friends and family party on around them.

I probably don't have to tell you this either, but I will. Make sure you don't have to travel far from the site of the wedding celebration on the night of your wedding. The idea of heading off to an exotic location is very enticing, but you'll be far better off if you book a room nearby for after the wedding party and then head out to Hawaii or Jamaica or Cabo San Lucas the next day or even two days later when you are fully recovered from all of the stress and excitement.

We were booked into a hotel room just a few miles away from the Trump venue for our wedding night. After thanking all of our guests and saying goodnight, we jumped into a car with a driver and headed for the hotel. We'd only driven a mile or so when Kanae realized she'd forgotten her suitcase. We didn't want to turn around and go back, so Kanae tried to call her mom on her cell phone to ask her to bring the suitcase.

The cell phone reception was bad, and as we were trying to call Kanae's mom, our driver slowed down on the narrow, winding road, thinking he might have to turn around. For some reason, this attracted the attention of a police officer who flipped on his red lights and ordered us to pull over!

The police officer walked up to the car, and Kanae rolled down her window. He saw that she was in her wedding gown and that brought a smile to his face.

"I'm not going to ruin your wedding night," he said, "so please tell your driver not to drive so slowly on this road. Congratulations and good night!"

And so we did not spend our honeymoon night in the county jail, thus avoiding our first potential disaster, and arrest, as man and wife.

Nine

The Joys of Abstinence Before Marriage and Sex After Marriage

*W*e know this can be a serious and touchy subject, and sexual abstinence is also a very personal matter, so we are only sharing our thoughts and experience on the topic. We are not trying to make anyone feel uncomfortable or guilty, and we are not telling you what you must do. That's not our business. We can only tell you what our views are and what was right for us according to our faith.

Having noted all of the above, I have to share a funny story with you on this topic. When a friend asked Kanae if putting off sex with me until after our marriage was difficult, she replied, "Well, it sure helped that he doesn't have any hands!"

I cracked up laughing when she said that! I love my wife so much; she tells it like it is. Kanae's straightforward answer also reflects the fact that sexual abstinence before marriage can be very challenging for couples who love and desire each other. After all, love and desire are good things, and so is sex—within a marriage. Saving sexual intimacy until after the wedding is God's ideal for Christian couples, but that doesn't mean it's easy.

Living up to ideals can be difficult, especially this one, because of all the temptations, urges, and pressures. This is a personal decision and we don't judge others. We certainly struggled with it, but we were very glad we made the decision. And the challenges of abstinence before marriage were another reason we were very relieved that the police officer decided not to throw us in jail. It was difficult enough to experience any delay on the way to the hotel on our wedding night.

We were so close, yet so far!

If you are in love, planning on getting married, and struggling with abstaining from sex, please know that there is no reason to feel bad about your conflicting feelings and emotions. You should be commended for wanting to do the right thing. We really wanted to save sex for our married life. We were strongly attracted to each other, so abstinence was a challenge. After we became engaged, we were so excited and thrilled, and the temptation became even greater. We both prayed for God's strength in resisting temptation. We also considered getting married a lot sooner. I do recommend a short engagement period if you are holding off, and I'm not the only one who thinks that is a good idea.

When Kanae and I met the Reverend Billy Graham after our engagement, his advice was "Get married quick!" Reverend Graham understood the challenges and rewards of abstinence. Talking to him also helped me remember something that Uncle Batta said when Kanae and I began dating. He reminded me that as a Christian and an evangelist who preaches God's Word and encourages others to follow it, I should live it.

When I started dating Kanae, he grilled me with questions about my plans, my feelings for her, and what I was doing to remain abstinent. When he saw that Kanae and I were affectionate and snuggly, he offered to pray for us. I appreciated that, and I recommend you find people to pray for you if you are ever in a similar situation.

GETTING TO KNOW EACH OTHER

The Bible uses the term "to know" in referring to relationships between men and women. In a true loving relationship, you should take the time to know and understand each other before having sex. Many, but not all, men tend to view sex as merely a physical thing, a source of pleasure. But others, mostly women, take it as a sign of deep commitment to their partner.

The Bible is very clear about that. I've known a lot of people who move in together and have an intimate relationship before marrying. Some say it's necessary to get to know each other at that level before committing to marriage. On the other hand, author and Christian philosopher C. S. Lewis in his book *Mere Christianity,* likened sex without marriage to one who enjoys the pleasure of tasting food but does not want to swallow and digest it. He said sex is meant to be part of marriage and should not be separated from it, because both the marriage and the sex lose their meaning when that happens.

Kanae also said something that makes a lot of sense: Many young people have sex before marriage because they think they've met the one they'll be with for the rest of their life. But how often does "the one" turn out to be the *wrong* one? A lot of teens and adults have regrets about having sex when the relationship doesn't lead to marriage. Teens are especially vulnerable to the emotional toll this takes. Having sex creates the feeling that the other person is committed to you, but when it happens outside of marriage, that is mostly an illusion.

One in Spirit

Popular culture tends to portray sex as being all about emotional impulses and desire instead of something designed to bring a married couple together in a loving, beautiful, and spiritual way. Movies, certain forms of music, television shows, and novels also have a tendency to separate sex from any association with love, watering down its significance and importance. Those who are sexually active before marriage miss out on the richness of the true gift, which is beyond temporary pleasure. I found that there are many reasons to wait and many layers to this gift.

Scripture says when you have sex, you become one in spirit, and that was how God designed sex to be in a marriage. Once you become one in the flesh with someone, you are then spiritually one as well. That is why many people feel like a part of them has left them forever when they have sex with someone and the relationship doesn't go any further. They feel as though something's been lost or taken from them.

If that has happened to you, my advice is to take a vow of abstinence until you find the love of your life, and then make a commitment with that person to save sex for your life as a married couple. You may have made mistakes and slipped up in the past, but you can begin anew! We all fail now and then in one way or another—and often in many ways. Ask for God's forgiveness and strength, and then forgive yourself and vow to do better when you find the right person. What's important is that you and the person you plan to marry set boundaries and agree to share yourselves only after you've entered into a partnership blessed by God.

Sex without marriage is not authentic in our view, because there is no true commitment to each other or to God. Some singles feel they'll miss out on something if they don't have sex before marriage, but casual sex involves taking something beautiful and intended to reflect God's love and turning it into something that is selfish and empty. I believe you shouldn't be with someone physically unless you are committed to being with that person emotionally and spiritually. And when I say committed, I mean married.

I've heard people talk about feeling a sense of emptiness and disorientation after having casual sex, and I think that's because God intended sex to be part of a committed marriage. Casual sex is like buying a fake Gucci watch for five bucks from a guy on the street. It looks like a Gucci and feels like a Gucci, but you will always know it's a fake. You just know there's something not quite right.

Casual sex before marriage also can be disorienting because it creates a false sense of intimacy. I've known men and women who are reluctant to walk away from a bad relationship mostly because they'd given themselves sexually to the other person. I've also known people who have had difficulty committing to a new relationship because they'd had sex with someone who later betrayed their trust or refused to commit to marriage.

Desire can be so powerful that you may feel you love a person even if the attraction is merely physical. The initial passion of a relationship is wonderful, but over time it fades. Too often, people realize that they aren't really in love with the other person, and they may realize they don't even like them.

That is why it is so important to establish deeper bonds by making sure there is more than mere physical attraction. Sex can make it difficult for you to know whether your bonds are strong enough to last once the passion diminishes.

THIS IS NOT A TEST DRIVE

You have probably heard the argument that having sex before marriage is necessary so that you know whether you are physically compatible. That may make sense until you realize that such an attitude turns what is supposed to be a loving, intimate, and exhilarating shared experience into a performance test. How loving, fun, and intimate is it to have sex just to "prove" you are compatible or that you can satisfy each other? That seems cold to me.

The same holds true of living together before you are married just to show that you can get along. How much fun is it to live together if the whole purpose is to test drive your relationship? How natural can you be with each other if you feel like every move you make is being judged and analyzed? What if you spill wine on her couch or gain ten pounds during the trial run? Will your test-drive partner head out the door?

Living together and having sex before marriage can put a relationship on tricky ground. Can you really be yourself if you are constantly trying to prove you are worthy of loving and marrying? When you are married, on the other hand, you grant each other acceptance. You love each other in good times and bad, in sickness and health. You have permission to be imperfect. To me, that's a much more enjoyable way to live.

Of course there is also the concern that an unplanned pregnancy could result from sex outside of marriage. It's challenging enough to have a child when you are married, but the challenges increase exponentially when there is no legally binding commitment. Now, it's true that many single parents do a great job raising their children, but most will tell you that it is not easy and that they probably would have chosen a different set of circumstances for their children.

The reality is that some who become pregnant outside of marriage decide to have an abortion. They may go on with their lives, but this is an act that comes with lifelong repercussions.

Premarital sex also makes you even more vulnerable to being hurt and feeling betrayed because there is no long-term commitment. That is easier to understand intellectually than to deal with physically, I know. Though I lack arms and legs, believe me, I have desires like every other man. Kanae is a beautiful woman. It took God's grace, a lot of prayer, and all of my strength of will as a Christian—as well as her own determination and faith—to keep us apart before marriage.

As Christians, we know that when we honor God in our lives, He honors and protects us. If we live according to His Word, we reap the blessings. God is good. Even when we do wrong, God is good and His kindness, love, and forgiveness are there for all who seek Him.

What a beautiful blessing it was that just three months after our wedding

Kanae became pregnant with Kiyoshi. So our wonderful baby boy, who was born a year and a day after our wedding, was one of the greatest rewards we will ever receive. We believe our blessing came to us because Kanae and I entered into our marriage knowing that we did our best to establish and honor boundaries for our relationship during our courtship.

Living Your Beliefs

Kanae and I are also honored to serve as examples for my sister, Michelle, and her fiancé, Daniel, who became engaged in early 2014. A few months into their engagement, Michelle posted a picture of them hugging, and the words "Worth the Wait" were written (in washable ink) on her hand to display their commitment to abstinence from sex until their marriage.

Michelle and Daniel, whose parents are longtime missionaries in Zimbabwe, fell in love after just one date, but they also declared their boundaries to each other on that same date. I know they will face temptations just as Kanae and I did, so we will pray for them, encourage them, and support them in every way we can.

We would like to share with you some of the advice we've offered Michelle and Daniel. Again, we don't hold ourselves up to be perfect examples in any way. In fact, we hold ourselves up to be imperfect, not only because that is true, but also because no one is perfect. We understand that!

We acknowledge that once we fell for each other, the temptations were a constant battle. Kanae and I are very affectionate and expressive by nature. After all, I once set the Guinness World Record for most hugs in one hour— 1,749 to be exact! During our courtship, Kanae and I wanted to be as close as possible at all times. We were always touching, holding, and kissing each other, but we always kept in mind that we had to maintain the boundaries we both believed in. So we worked out some ways to keep it cool, even when we were feeling the heat of passion.

Here, then are...

Nick and Kanae's Ten Tips for Keeping It Cool Before Marriage

1. Buddy up! In the old days, courting couples were accompanied by a chaperone who made sure there was no hanky-panky in the backseat of the horse carriage. Rather than bring back the designated nag, we tried to double date or go out in groups with others committed to abstinence to help reduce temptation. We spent a lot of time with family members, including our parents, which also helped us to bond with each other's relatives.

2. I have mixed feelings about making faith or God the wet blanket, but it can be helpful to remember that the person you are with isn't yours to own or possess. The one you adore is a child of God and should be treated with respect, which includes respecting moral beliefs and boundaries and not leading the person into temptation.

3. When we did spend time alone on dates, we tried to keep it wholesome by avoiding racy movies, videos, television shows, and music. We looked for Christian programming or other uplifting and inspiring entertainment.

4. Get out in the open. We spent much of our courtship outdoors, on the beach, on a boat, having picnics, by the pool, and in parks where we could enjoy each other's company and the surroundings while limiting physical contact to hugs and kisses.

5. Avoid alcohol and any drugs that reduce inhibitions and cloud judgment. This is just common sense, of course. We all know that

drinking and drugs are not the friend of abstinence. A glass of wine now and then may be okay, but too often one glass leads to another… and another, and then comes temptation.

6. If you feel your passions heating up, take a break, remind yourselves of the boundaries and goals you have set, and pray for moral strength. Cold showers are also recommended, but not together! I'm sorry.

7. Keep the lights on! I'm told that back in my father's time there was a "both feet on the floor" rule when couples were alone in a room together. That obviously would not work for me, but keeping the lights on and other people around proved to be a good strategy. On occasion, Kanae had to bind me to a heavy chair with duct tape, but that was necessary only three or four or seventeen times. (*Kidding!*)

8. Find nonphysical ways to show your affection. Kanae cooked for me quite a bit during our courtship, and as a result, in a very short time she had even more of me to love. I gained ten pounds! She is an excellent cook, and she views preparing meals for me as a show of her love and affection. In return, I wrote songs and poems to her, took her on trips, surprised her with gifts and flowers, and planned little adventures so we could be together but not fall into temptation.

9. Remind yourselves that you are abstaining only for a short time and for long-term reasons. Kanae and I found that if we talked at least once a week about how soon we would be married and free to be together, it helped us to stay focused on that goal. We discussed the benefits of waiting and how good it would feel to be able to tell our children that we saved this part of our relationship for our wedding night and our life together as a married couple. It was important to me also to be able to recommend abstinence to teens in my speeches without feeling like a hypocrite. So that also served as an incentive.

10. Did I mention cold showers and duct tape already? I hope you laughed at that, because laughter is another great, nonsexual way to bond with your future spouse. When I think about the happiest and most secure married couples I know, nearly all of them laugh and joke and tease each other frequently. Kanae often says that we laughed more during our courtship than we do as a married couple. I agree, and I think we need to fix that. I always want us to be able to see the humor in life, and to remind ourselves that we are on this earth to be joyful together.

THE JOY OF ABSTINENCE—AND SEX

There is something joyful and comforting to knowing that on your wedding night, you and your spouse are starting out together without having past experiences cloud your intimacy. It's a very special thing to share that first time together as God intended it, within marriage.

Kanae and I believe that God's way is the best way. That's not to say that He won't forgive you if you mess up. He forgives if you ask for forgiveness and healing. God is a merciful God. If you honor the Lord, His blessings will be in abundance in your life.

Now it's time we had The Talk.

Not the talk you had with your parents or minister about sex when you were a teenager; this is a different sort of talk. In my readings about sexual abstinence and in my discussions with other Christians, I've learned of an after-effect that concerns me, even though it's quite understandable.

There are men and women who convince themselves not to have sex before marriage by deciding that sex itself is a bad thing—dirty, disgusting, or evil. Even when they marry, they have difficulty shedding this view of sex, and as a result, they either refuse to have sex or only do it rarely and out of a sense of duty. That's just wrong.

Sex is a wonderful gift that connects a husband and wife in service to each other. It is a shared blessing that keeps a marriage healthy and whole. This gift is part of the marriage covenant and your vow to become one as God intended.

He created men and women, and the different ways in which they were configured wasn't an accident. They were made to have sex together as both a means of uniting as one and as a means of reproduction. We are sexual creatures. When we marry and express our love by joining our bodies together, we are honoring our Creator and His plan for us.

Bible scholars describe the Song of Solomon as a poem about sexual love as a source of pleasure and shared intimacy—a gift from God that helps bring married couples closer together. Sex between a man and wife is not evil. It's not dirty. It's not disgusting. In fact, it is such a beautiful and wondrous gift from God that it should be reserved for and shared with the person you are committed to for the rest of your life. God made sex for marriage, and it is something holy and sacred in that context. Many Christian scholars and teachers say that sex between man and wife is a reflection of the joy and oneness in spirit that comes from being one with God through Christ. That is why you wait. You don't abstain from premarital sex because sex itself is bad. When a married couple has sex, they are doing what God intended and what the Bible condones. Once you are married, sex isn't about performance or trying to impress anyone. It's about pleasing each other, sharing intimacy, trusting, and, yes, enjoying your physical, emotional, and spiritual bonds.

I would advise all men and women to continue to be thoughtful in their approach to sex even after they are married. There will be times when you won't be on the same page as far as when and how you want to have sex. These are issues that need to be worked out in a considerate, empathetic, and kind way. The demands of work, children, and other pressing distractions can pose challenges to a couple's sex life. I encourage you not to harbor resentment and frustration but to instead talk through issues on this delicate matter and to always be gentle and loving with each other.

Sex should never be withheld as a punishment. It is meant to be an act of mutual consent that strengthens your bonds, not something that drives you apart. As the scripture goes, don't ever go to bed angry or with unresolved issues. If nothing else, you can agree to disagree, or you can agree to discuss and resolve the issue in the morning.

Kanae and I love each other so much that our physical desire for each other was never a question. Once we both proclaimed our love for each other and we were headed toward marriage, I made it a point to assure her that my physical imperfections did not include anything that would prohibit or interfere with our ability to have sex once we were married.

She hadn't asked, but I wanted to dispel any questions or doubts she might have had. Believe me, I've been dealing with being asked such questions from childhood into adulthood. I've been asked every sort of invasive personal question you might imagine—and some you'd never think of, I assure you.

Still, I never expected a television reporter to delve into my most private information on the air. But it happened during an interview when Kanae was pregnant. A female reporter in Dallas asked me during a live television interview how it was possible for us to have a child. I was more than a little flustered by her question. I tried to put her off by saying, "Well, most people know you don't need arms and legs to have a child."

That didn't seem to deter her. She asked again, saying people were curious as to how I could become a father. At that point, I realized she was serious. I could have replied in a way that put her down for going too far into our personal life with her inquiries. Instead, I went for humor.

So on live television I said, "Actually, I hear that legs sometimes just get in the way!" Believe me, that put a stop to her personal questions.

On another occasion, Kanae and I were interviewed together on *60 Minutes Australia,* and the interviewer, my friend Peter Overton, respectfully asked about intimacy issues.

Kanae replied, "Well, I mean, Nick has everything he needs…"

Good one, babe!

Ten

When Two Become One

few months after Kanae and I were married, I had a business trip scheduled in Los Angeles. We live a couple of hours from the hotel where the meeting was to take place. I planned to have my caregiver drive me into Los Angeles, conduct the meeting, and then return later that afternoon.

When I told Kanae about my plan, she looked very sad. I don't like it when my wife looks sad.

"What's wrong, baby?" I asked.

"You didn't even ask me if I wanted to go with you," she replied with tears in her eyes. *Husband failure alert!*

Strangely enough, just before this happened, I'd come across a line in the Bible that said, "When a man has taken a new wife, he shall not go out to war or be charged with any business; he shall be free at home one year, and bring happiness to his wife whom he has taken." I had thought that was a pretty good rule when I read it, maybe not very practical in the modern world, but a good idea nonetheless. Then I went and broke it!

As much fun as it might be, it's just not possible for most newly married men to take a year off from work to "bring happiness" to their wives these days. But I think all married couples could benefit from approaching marriage from the beginning as the opportunity to bring happiness to each other.

That sounds very noble doesn't it? Maybe a little naive? Well, that all depends on how you feel about the person you married. If you aren't willing to make adjustments to accommodate the needs and desires of your spouse, my guess is that the marriage will either be a brief one or a very unhappy one.

When I planned my quick trip into Los Angeles without thinking to invite Kanae to come along, I was operating like premarital Nick. I was taking care of business and myself without adjusting for the fact that I was no longer a one-man show. It wasn't a major husband failure, but it was an early warning sign that I had not sufficiently adjusted my thought processes from SGM (single guy mode) to MGM (married guy mode).

I actually had thought about asking her, but then I thought she probably had better things to do. I hadn't thought about working in a little family time after the meeting to do something in Los Angeles, but apparently my wife had. I learned to be more thoughtful about taking opportunities to spend time with Kanae because even when you don't say it, your wife wants you to be thinking, *I want to be with you as much as I can.*

This, by the way, is a very common failing for newlyweds, both men and women, and it's understandable. I doubt if there has ever been a new husband or a new wife who didn't mess up at some point in the first few months of a marriage by not taking into consideration the feelings, needs, or desires of the spouse. This is why the Bible also reminds us to love our spouses as ourselves.

Is that even possible? Yes, I believe it is. In fact, I believe the best marriages are those in which both the husband and wife are pretty much dedicated to putting each other first. Oh, and by the way, I'm very aware that it's much easier to say that than to do it.

I am still learning what it takes to be a good husband, and it could be a long, long learning curve. Kanae's reaction to my plans to go solo to Los Angeles for the day was my first wake-up call. My wife was very sweet about my slip-up, actually. She said she just wanted to be with me as much as possible. Her tears melted my heart.

I realized that after more than twenty-five years as a single bloke, there is quite an adjustment to the married man mind-set. I needed to take more literally the "two become one" concept and keep in mind at all times that it's no longer just about me.

Many of my married male friends say they have had to make the same shift in their thinking, especially those who didn't get married until they'd been out in the world a few years on their own. Single guys get used to going their own way, doing what they want to do when they want to do it. But you can't be that self-centered and have a happy marriage. I believe you have to put your relationship first. Someone once told me the secret isn't to focus on yourself less, it's to care about your spouse more.

A GIVING MARRIAGE

I know someone who desperately wants to get married. She feels she's at the age when it's expected of women. She's told me several times that she wants to find a husband who will love her, give her financial security, and make her happy. I respect her and I understand her feelings, but if she expects that getting married will make her happy, she should probably check with all the other married people out there.

Don't get me wrong, I am very happy to be married to Kanae. She and our son are the joys of my life. But I don't think you should demand that your spouse or your marriage provide your happiness. First of all, true happiness is generated from within. Second, I firmly believe that the best marriages are those in which both husband and wife are committed to making the relationship work by supporting and encouraging each other. It's all about the giving, not the receiving.

Making my wife happy makes me happy, of course, so I benefit from being a good husband. But I think marriage requires both husband and wife to sacrifice their self-interests for the good of the relationship. In 1 Corinthians 13, we're told, "Love suffers long and is kind; love does not envy; love does not parade itself, is not puffed up; does not behave rudely, does not seek its own."

Kanae's little wake-up call to me about being left out of my Los Angeles meeting plans served to remind me that I needed to make more of an adjustment from "me" to "we." Even though I intended to be a husband who puts his wife first, I wasn't living up to my ultimate role model as a Christian: Jesus, who humbly served our needs by dying on the cross.

Dropping Childish Ways

Unselfishness doesn't come naturally to most of us when we are young and sometimes not even when we reach adulthood. A little later in 1 Corinthians 13, we're reminded of the importance of adjusting our attitudes as our responsibilities increase: "When I was a child, I spoke as a child, I understood as a child, I thought as a child; but when I became a man, I put away childish things."

I think that passage can be applied to those entering marriage too. Once you enter into that holy union, you have to put aside your childish, self-centered ways and adjust to a new attitude and a new perspective. You have to let go of self-interest, but at the same time, I think it's also essential that both the husband and wife go deeper in self-knowledge.

It's a bit of a joke among newly married men that they never knew they had so many flaws until their wives started pointing them out. Part of this is simply adjusting to living with another person and having to be more considerate. Anyone who has ever had a roommate knows that adjustments have to be made.

There is also the matter of baggage. Most of us get married with personal baggage of some sort—and I'm not referring to American Tourister or Gucci bags. Many men and women come to marriage with insecurities related to previous relationships that didn't work out. Or, they might have grown up in a broken or dysfunctional family that has left them with trust issues.

We may not even be aware of the baggage that burdens us, but we can carry into our marriages resentments, mistrust, and sensitivities that have nothing to do with our spouses. After we are married and conflict occurs, we may overreact or lash out based not on what is happening in the marriage necessarily but on past hurts from previous relationships that have left us feeling vulnerable.

We like to think we're not hampered by baggage from our past, but most of us are lugging it around whether we realize it or not. When Kanae said yes to my marriage proposal, I was over the moon with excitement and joy. One of the thoughts that played in my mind in the months before our marriage was that finally I was free of my lifelong insecurities, particularly my fear that no woman would want to marry a man without limbs.

Then, just a year or so into our marriage, a friend asked me if I ever reflected back on those old insecurities now that I was happily married to a lovely woman. He was surprised at my answer. He thought I'd be more secure—and so did I before getting married—but it hasn't worked out that way.

"You know, I'd gotten used to being a single guy with no arms and no legs, but I'm still getting used to being a married guy with no arms and no legs," I told him.

BAGGAGE PROBLEMS

After the excitement of the wedding wore off and we settled into daily life together, I was shocked to discover that many of my old insecurities about my lack of limbs had returned. The feelings were very raw, in fact. I couldn't figure it out at first, but then I realized something. When I was single and living alone, I could do almost anything I needed to do on my own, or I had people working for me who could do those things I was unable to do.

But once Kanae and I were living together, it bothered me a great deal that she had to do certain "husband chores," like taking out the garbage. It also bugged me that I couldn't cook for her or help her wash the dishes. Suddenly, I was being reminded on a regular basis of my shortcomings. I thought I'd grown out of those feelings, but those insecurities grew worse when Kiyoshi was born and I couldn't pick him up and hold him when he was crying. It really bothered me that I couldn't relieve Kanae of some of the parenting duties so she could get the rest she needed so badly.

Now, what I didn't realize at first was that my insecurities were causing frustration and making me very edgy. When something arose and I couldn't handle it like a "normal" husband, I tended to growl at Kanae, who couldn't understand why I was being irritable toward her.

Does this sound familiar? It's the old unseen baggage scenario, and it plays out in most marriages in varying forms. Kanae had a similar experience in a different situation. Before we were married, I got into a heated argument one night with my brother, Aaron. Everything really was fine between us; we were just doing what brothers sometimes do. But I was shocked to see that Kanae was emotionally affected by our argument.

When Kanae and I talked through it later, I realized that she is very sensitive to my raising my voice because of her childhood experiences. As the child of parents who divorced, she knew what arguments could lead to in a marriage.

If you look at our wedding pictures, you cannot see either of us carrying baggage down the aisle, but apparently it was there. In fact, I remembered just recently that when we were leaving the ceremony after our joyous exchange of wedding vows, I became frustrated because I couldn't reach down and pick up the train of Kanae's wedding dress, which people were accidentally stepping on.

That frustration was just an early hint that being married would rekindle some of those feelings of helplessness that I thought I'd overcome since childhood.

We all have baggage of some sort, of course. Your marriage won't be burdened by it if you recognize those feelings exist and make the necessary adjustments. It helps to be mindful of your emotions and control your response to them so that your spouse doesn't become your unwitting whipping post. It's another adjustment men and women need to make when they become a couple bound by holy matrimony. If you don't adjust, marriage can become an unholy war, and nobody wants that, right?

A Change in the Game Plan

I'm a big soccer fan. In fact, I was practically an All-World Living Room Soccer Star back in my childhood. One of the things that is true about soccer and nearly every other sport is that coaches have to adjust their strategies as the game plays out. Sometimes their original game plans haven't taken into consideration roster changes or new offensive and defensive plays introduced by the opponent. So those coaches and players who can adjust to the new realities are usually the most successful.

I believe the same thing applies to marriages. We have to adjust our expectations and our actions to the changes brought by marriage, especially in the early years when we are setting the boundaries and tone of our lives together. From what I've seen, read, and been told, I believe it is a continuous process of adjusting to each other's needs, desires, and feelings. But it's important to always do this with the spirit of putting the other person first—not because you have to, but because you want to.

Many couples enter into marriage expecting to find happiness, serenity, and fulfillment, but they often discover that the fast pace of modern life makes it difficult for them to spend as much time together as they need to stay close.

It's often a challenge to meet those high expectations due to the demands of work and parenting. One study found that spouses who spent time talking or doing something together at least once a week were 3.5 times more likely to be happy in their marriage than those who spent less time interacting one-on-one.

In other words, if you don't put in the time, your marriage won't be worth a dime. (Yes, I made that up. I'm a poet, but my feet don't show it!) Kanae and I have learned that it's hard on our marriage when I am gone for long periods. We lose touch with each other even if we talk on the phone or Skype every day. As a result, I'm always looking for ways to travel less or to take Kanae and Kiyoshi with me. We believe that being together as much as possible is necessary to get what we both want out of our marriage.

TIME TOGETHER

Kanae has helped me to understand the importance of time spent together in ways I never would have figured out on my own. Mostly, she serves as an example of what a loving partner should be. She is one of the most unselfish, giving, and naturally caring people I've ever known. I've already given you a couple of examples of this. One was the Nick-friendly wrapping job she did on a gift she gave me. Another was her admonishment that I should never apologize for asking her to do something for me. A third was the wonderful wedding cake bride and groom she created all on her own.

Every day, in many ways, Kanae expresses her love for me. She is also not afraid to tell me when I need to make an adjustment so that she feels the same love coming from me that I feel coming from her. Most of what she wants from me—and I'm sure many spouses feel this way—is my time, attention, and understanding.

Here's Kanae's take on it.

꩜

If Nick and I don't talk and spend time together each day, our relationship suffers. God gave Nick a brain that is always working. He comes up with new ideas and projects constantly. He even talks about his ideas in his sleep! It's a blessing to have a brain like that, but it can be a challenge, too, because it's sometimes difficult to get him to focus on more personal issues like our relationship and just relaxing and laughing and spending time together. I have to remind him to do that sometimes, because he gets so caught up in creating opportunities and making the most of them.

FOCUSING ON THE RELATIONSHIP

Before I found Kanae and we were married, I couldn't understand what married people meant when they said that marriage can be hard work. I just didn't see how being with someone you love and desire took that sort of effort. It didn't take me long to understand once I was married, however. It's not work so much as focus that is required. My speaking career, evangelism, books, videos, and other projects require a great deal of time and attention. While I've tried to cut down on my travels since we married, I still spend many hours in planes, buses, trains, and cars.

Even when Kanae and I are alone together, it's often difficult for me to turn off my work thoughts and focus instead on my wife and our relationship. I know this is a challenge for many married couples, especially when both spouses have a busy life consumed by work and family demands.

We went to dinner with an older married couple recently, and the wife told us that they hadn't taken time for a vacation in many years because they were so busy with their careers and family matters. The wife said it had gotten to the sad point that even when they were alone, they had lost the ability to talk to each other about their feelings and their relationship.

They tried to break the pattern by attending a couples retreat and seeing a marriage therapist, but they'd become so disconnected that they feared their marriage might not survive. I think they were trying to warn us that if you don't grow together, you grow apart.

Kanae and I took her warning to heart. It's something all couples should think about no matter how long they've been married. You can't take each other for granted. You have to show your love and appreciation not just with flowers and greeting cards on your anniversary, birthday, and Valentine's Day, but every day through your actions. Basically, you have to pay attention to your marriage, just as you pay attention to your career and your children.

If you pay attention and make adjustments when you see something is lacking or needs to be addressed, your marriage will be more likely to grow richer and more rewarding over the years. If you don't pay attention and adjust to changing circumstances, your relationship and your marriage may suffer and even come to an end.

My wife is so wise. Sometimes I think she's much older than she claims to be—an "old" spirit in a young body. When I discussed this topic with her recently, she cited a passage in the Bible that says, "For where your treasure is, there your heart will be also." She believes the word "treasure" refers to the things you spend the most time on—your work, your relationships, your faith, and whatever you are passionate about. Here's more of what she had to say about that, and some of her interesting observations on the difference between our courtship and our marriage.

I can see how easy it is to get so carried away with work or other urgent and demanding things that you can lose focus on your marriage and your relationship. But we have to not only make time for each other but also focus on each other's needs, desires, and emotions so we can serve each other. A marriage can become very fragile if you don't pay attention, invest your time and effort, and make adjustments when needed.

And isn't it funny how when people date, they do all the things couples are supposed to do? They spend lots of time together. I mean, every minute possible, and if they aren't in the same place, they are constantly texting, e-mailing, and talking on the phone to each other. They really work at keeping close and having meaningful conversations—even the silent times together are special because they are so focused on loving and caring for each other. They go on dates and do adventurous things. They are romantic. They want to please each other and show their best side, while also promising to be better for each other.

Then, when a couple marries, things too often shift back from "we" to "me." We are very selfless while dating, and yet we tend to become selfish in marriage, always thinking about our individual needs and desires instead of serving each other. I think we can all do better at marriage if we bring some of that dating attitude to our daily life as a couple—as "we" instead of "me."

I have realized that after being single much of my life, there is quite an adjustment to the married man's mind-set. Our premarital classes, given by the pastor who married us, included the message that marriage was designed as a mutual submission. The husband and wife give their lives to each other. I think that because affairs and divorce have become so common, many couples give up on marriage rather than putting in more effort to improve the relationship and build upon it. Yet a marriage in which both people are fully committed and focused on each other's needs can be incredibly rewarding and satisfying. Whenever possible, Kanae and I pray together and read the Bible every day, because we know we need God's help in keeping our marriage strong.

We also have learned to take the time as often as we are able to share our feelings and concerns so that we can make adjustments as we go along. If the choice is all out or all in, we want to be all in, striving every day for a better marriage, a stronger relationship, and a greater bond so that we can know and serve each other according to God's will.

PRIORITY ADJUSTMENT

Kanae and I are still working on "the work" of marriage. By that I mean we are still figuring out what it takes to keep the bonds of love and respect strong. Part of that is learning what each of us wants and expects from our relationship and our marriage. I mentioned earlier that Kanae told me she doesn't think we laugh as much together as we did when we were dating. When I thought about it, I had to admit she was right, and that bothered me.

Being married and having a family can weigh heavily on both the man and wife, of course. I come from an old-school Serbian family in which the man was considered the breadwinner and the main source of financial support for the family. I think that responsibility has weighed on me more than I realized since we have been married. I can't ignore the necessity of supporting my wife and child, of course, but I need to put Serious Nick in the coat closet when I come home so we can enjoy the fruits of our labors and the blessings in our lives.

That's an adjustment I'm committed to making. The important thing is to understand that you can't take your relationship for granted even when you are married—make that *especially* when you are married. Your wife or husband has made a major commitment in marrying you, and if you don't honor that commitment by making that person a priority, what does that say to your spouse?

Kanae and I are still rookies when it comes to being married, but we have come up with some suggestions about "the work" involved in marriage maintenance once you've walked down the aisle and committed to each other. Here are…

NICK AND KANAE'S FIVE ROOKIE TIPS TO WORKING AT MARRIAGE

1. Sorry, but There Is No Coasting

Whether you got married just months after a brief but intense courtship or you have been in love since sitting next to each other in first grade, there may be a strong temptation to take each other for granted in the first months and years of marriage. It's understandable. You put a lot of effort into proving your love and worthiness to each other, and you may just feel like putting it on cruise control for a while.

The thing about cruise control is that it only works if traffic and road conditions never change, but change is inevitable on the interstate and in life. There is also the fact that when you marry someone, you don't lower the stakes of a relationship, you raise them. You become interdependent in every way, from your shared physical and emotional needs to your shared financial security. So you have to pay attention. If you don't, you can be sure your spouse—or life itself—will at some point deliver a wake-up call.

2. Conflicts Will Occur

You and your spouse may be two peas in a pod, as compatible as peanut butter and jelly, but sooner or later your wedded bliss will be disrupted. The conflict might be triggered by in-law family members or out-law friends. It may be circumstances beyond your control, or the fact that you refuse to hang up your wet bath towel. Prepare for it by keeping this in mind: Being right isn't nearly as important as being together. Sometimes you will be the windshield. Other times you will be the bug.

3. You Must Adjust

Marriage conflicts are inevitable. They only become crises when you don't make adjustments to resolve them. If you want your marriage to work, we suggest that you simply accept from the start that when conflicts occur—and they will—that the important thing isn't to win. Instead, you each should identify the problem from your perspective, find common ground, and then agree to make the necessary adjustments.

Sometimes this will mean simply accepting that "it is what it is" and letting go of resentments, anger, and the right to be right. The famous love passage in 1 Corinthians 13 tells us that along with being patient and kind, "love...thinks no evil." Some translations say that it keeps no record of wrongs. That's the Scripture version of "fuggedaboutit," as movie mobsters say. In other words, don't take conflicts personally; use them as opportunities to make your bonds stronger. Let go of hurtful feelings and focus on making the marriage better, not bitter.

4. Remember Why You Married Your Spouse in the First Place

I have a friend who, like me, married a younger woman who is also very smart, strong-willed, and not afraid to speak her mind. One day, their college-age son was present when my friend's wife let him have it for something he'd done that she did not like. After she vented, my friend turned to his son and calmly said with a smile, "Son, this is what comes with marrying a strong woman!"

I love this story, because it goes to the core of a married relationship. We choose the people we marry. My friend married a strong woman, and he knew that she would be a strong wife. He was willing to accept that when she had a bone to pick with him, she would not mince her words. He loved her strength, and he accepted it for better and for worse.

When Kanae and I are at odds, I find it very helpful to look beyond the conflict at hand to the woman I fell in love with. Then I remind myself that I vowed to honor her and keep her in good times and bad. Our love is bigger than any disagreements we might have. Our relationship is more important to me than being right or winning an argument.

I also try to step back and think about the fact that I was a very lonely single guy, and this woman has brought more joy into my life than I thought I'd ever know. That attitude, along with prayer, helps me get through the challenging times as a husband. Maybe it will help you too.

5. You Aren't in This Alone

There may be times when you just can't figure out your spouse. You may not be able to understand why there is a conflict, what you did wrong, or how to get beyond an issue that has put you at odds. In these moments, you may feel that you are all alone. After all, the person you love the most is the same person who is angry with you, right?

These are the times when you reach out for help and support. You could go to your family and friends, but before you do that, ask yourself if you really want to share your conflicts and frustration with them. They may feel it necessary to pick sides, and that can become an issue down the road.

Instead, you might want to consider talking with your minister, a marriage counselor, a therapist, or some other impartial third party with experience in relationship issues. And, most of all, talk to God and ask Him to give you wisdom and strength. In fact, my advice is to pray for His guidance and support each and every day—and maybe more often when you need help with this very important part of your life. Remember that if you can't change your spouse, God can. But also keep in mind that the person who may need to change could be you, and God will see that before you do!

Eleven

We're Having a Baby!

*A*fter our wedding and honeymoon, I became the man with a plan—a family plan, that is. We wanted to take the next two years and enjoy being husband and wife before trying to start a family. Kanae and I were excited at that prospect, especially because my staff had been planning a major worldwide speaking tour for 2013, with visits to over twenty countries.

After so many years of traveling solo, I was thrilled that Kanae would be accompanying me on this trip. Okay, I admit it: I wanted to show off my new bride to the world. Can you blame me?

Then once again, I was reminded of the old saying, "Man plans and God laughs."

In May, three months after our wedding, Kanae and I were camping out with about fifty middle school students and their chaperones at Camp Whittier in the Los Padres National Forest, north of Santa Barbara, California. We weren't exactly roughing it at this beautiful place, with two lodges and nineteen cabins on fifty-five acres along Cachuma Lake.

It was a leadership retreat for teens put together by my team at Attitude Is Altitude. The idea was to give me a lot of time with the campers. We had workshops, discussion groups, game challenges, and a lot of fun outdoor activities like high and low rope courses, wall climbing, and hiking.

The idea was to help our young campers think about what it means to be a leader, to help them identify their leadership abilities, and to give them fresh challenges so they could test their character and experience new levels of self-understanding and self-confidence.

Sounds great, right?

I was supposed to be the featured speaker, designated motivator, and all around camper in chief during this three-day funfest. During the event, I had no idea that I would soon be called upon to demonstrate my own strength of character, step out of my own comfort zone, and experience my own breakthrough.

LIFE CHANGER

You see, it was around this time that Kanae hinted about being a little worried because her body seemed to be off its usual schedule for her monthly cycle. We'd been traveling around, doing workshops and seminars and speeches, and she'd been hoping that maybe her body's timing was just out of whack because of all the excitement.

She kept hoping until she'd gone eleven days beyond her usual schedule. When we finally were home for a couple of days, my new wife went to the drugstore and bought a home pregnancy test. We hadn't been trying to start a family. In fact, we'd been trying *not* to start a family, so she wasn't real concerned—until the test strip results appeared.

Kanae recalls, "I saw the red lines and I stared at them a couple of seconds before blurting out, 'You are kidding me!' It wasn't a light pink; it was a strong dark red, so it wasn't like, 'Well, maybe, maybe not.' This was a pretty clear yes!"

Kanae came out of the bathroom and leaned against the wall in the hallway of our home. I found her there, holding the test strip in her hand, staring at it in disbelief.

"Baby, we are going to have a baby," she whispered.

Joy overwhelmed me for the first few minutes. I could not speak. Tears flowed. We hugged and kissed.

Then, as the reality of this news sank in, we had a bit of a zombie moment. We both went to our bed and crawled in, lying side by side, staring at the ceiling. Neither of us said a word for about twenty minutes. I don't know about Kanae, but there were so many thoughts bombarding my brain I couldn't have said anything if I wanted to. My circuits were overloaded.

Here are two of the first flashes that went careening around in my head like racecars on the Indy 500 track:

Oh, my God, I'm going to be a father, and that's incredible!

Oh, my God, I just signed off on the contracts for speeches and stadiums for the four-month world tour that starts in…eight months!

Meanwhile, lying next to me, Kanae's mind was whirling just as fast as my own. I could hear all the clicks, buzzes, whirls, whoops, and shrieks coming from inside her brain. Oddly enough, the first thing she said to me was, "You are going to have to tell Karla to hurry up, because I don't want to be pregnant alone."

She and our friend, Karla Mills, who is chief operating officer of Attitude Is Altitude, had been talking about wanting to have a baby at the same time "someday." But I didn't need to call Karla and tell her to hurry up. Later that same day, I called her to see if we could change some of the tour appearance dates because they were on our baby's projected birth date. I didn't tell Karla the reason, but she knows me all too well. She could tell I was flustered and immediately guessed why: "Are you guys pregnant?"

"Yep," I said.

"That's awesome! So am I!"

No Piece of Cake

Kanae and I might have stayed in our zombie state for the entire day if we hadn't previously invited my father, mother, and sister over for dinner. Kanae had to get cooking.

"Are we going to tell them tonight?" Kanae asked.

I didn't think we had much choice. It's a well-known fact in our family that I am terrible at keeping secrets. (Note to the reader: If you ever plan on robbing a bank, do not tell me!)

Once we agreed to make our big announcement at the dinner with my family, Kanae turned on her creative artsy-craftsy imagination to come up with a memorable way to break the baby news.

"How about if you order a special cake that has blue icing on one side and pink icing on the other?" she suggested. "Then, when we serve it and go to cut it, we'll ask each person whether they want pink or blue, and see if they pick up on that?"

I ordered the cake and later in the afternoon, I drove to pick it up. While I was gone, Kanae decided to take one more home pregnancy test so she could be certain that we weren't about to break fake family news. This test also was positive, so we could go ahead and have our cake and eat it too. (Sorry, couldn't resist.)

Kanae's plan was to serve dinner, and then, when everyone was done, she would send my mum into the kitchen to get the cake. My wife envisioned my mother seeing the blue and pink icing, figuring out what that meant, and then rushing into the dining room, screaming in excitement with the baby cake in hand.

This plan made sense to me. My mother, after all, had been a delivery room nurse and midwife for many years. Surely she would see the cake and immediately know what it symbolized.

But surely, she didn't.

After dinner, Kanae sent mum in to get the cake. My mum walked out with it, plopped it on the dinner table, and said, "Okay, guys, go ahead. I'm not having dessert. I'm going to go out and water the sod; it's looking a little dry."

That's my mum for you; she can't sit still. She's always running around, doing this and that. She's a real busy bee and not very observant either.

Kanae looked at me like, "That wasn't the plan!"

By now you may have noticed that our plans don't often go very well.

With my wife about to have the first panic attack of her pregnancy, I tried to intercept my clueless mother. "Don't you want to have dessert?" I said, hinting with every trick I knew.

"No," she said.

It was time to take command. I'd spent three days training young leaders, so now I had to step up and be one. "Mum, please sit down and relax," I said. "Can you cut the cake for us please? You are so much better at it than me."

She didn't get the hint or the sarcasm, but she did sit down and began cutting the cake. (Mothers like it when they have something useful to do.)

To Kanae and me, the pink and blue cake was screaming "We're pregnant!" but no one else seemed to take notice. Mum cut the entire cake into neat and tidy pieces and then stood up. Apparently she planned to return to her important mission of watering our sod.

There seemed to be no stopping her, but I tried. "Mum! Please sit down and have family time with us." She's always been a sucker for family time.

Once we had her seated again, I tried dropping some bigger hints—hints the size of the *Hindenburg*. Everyone else was digging into their cake. My mother refused to take a slice.

"Okay, Mum, you don't have to eat, but if you were to pick a piece of cake, would you pick a pink one or a blue one?" I asked.

"Blue," she said.

Silence.

Hints were dropping like flies, but no one was picking them up.

We looked at Mum.

My mum looked at us.

Finally, I turned to Kanae in surrender. "Should we tell them?"

"You tell them," said Kanae.

"No, you tell them," I said. (I was afraid of breaking down in tears, but I'd never admit that.)

Kanae took the challenge. Bless her. "Well, we thought it would be obvious if we brought out a cake that was half blue and half pink, but apparently none of you got the hint…"

"You're pregnant!" my mother cried out. She is slow, but sure.

My father was even slower on the uptake. "What? WHAT? *You are what?*" he said.

My little sister was a bit quicker on her feet. Michelle was the first one up dancing, jumping up and down, and shrieking in joy, but Mum was quickly at her side doing a Serbian jig, if there is such a thing.

Okay, now I'll admit it: I cried.

They were so happy! We were so happy!

I was going to be a father!

BABY ON BOARD

So just ten hours after I learned that I was to be a father, we shared the news with my family: The first grandchild was on the way! It was a joyful moment, one of the warmest of my life. To see my parents and sister celebrating with my beautiful wife was one of those gifts I'll always remember.

Later that night, when my family had departed and Kanae was asleep beside me, I thought again about my journey away from my fears, insecurities, and loneliness to marriage and, now, impending fatherhood. I can't remember how old I was when I first told my mother that I wanted to have children one day. I do remember that she and my father seemed doubtful or wary in their responses whenever we spoke about that dream.

"Nick, we don't even know if you can have children," she'd said.

That hurt me a little, because I wanted to be thought of as a normal guy with normal desires and dreams and capabilities, despite my lack of limbs. I guess I hoped my parents felt the same way, but as I matured, I could better understand their caution.

My arrival was such a shock to them. It took my mother many months to deal with her grief. They had no clue what to do with me at first. They put themselves and their unique son in God's hands in the belief that where they were weak, He was strong.

They invested in me the same faith. I certainly struggled at times. As the realities of my disabilities became more and more apparent, I grieved too. I had to accept that there were so many normal things I could not do for myself, and that was very difficult. The teen years were especially difficult. Bullies preyed on me. Other kids avoided me. In those years when being accepted and fitting in is so important, I had more reason than most to feel like an outcast. No matter what I did, I would never look like everyone else.

My life as a lonely single guy seemed to drag on and on, and then God sent Kanae to me. The days flew by, our love took hold, and we were married. Now, only a few months into our marriage, we were blessed with this child. I could hardly believe this was real.

A Child for Us

I have read that God neither slumbers nor sleeps, which is a good thing, because if He did, Kanae and I would've kept Him up all night after we discovered we had a child on the way. We prayed to thank God, and we prayed for His delivery of a baby who would not have to deal with the same challenges presented to me.

We did consult with a doctor right away. I was assured that the odds of my fathering a child without limbs were astronomical. Not that it would be the worst thing in the world. Who better to serve as parents to such a child than me and the woman who loves me? Besides, I think no arms and no legs is no problem. Well, at least it's no problem that can't be handled with a lot of determination, faith, and family support.

Kanae and I talked about this at length. I believe God created me to serve as a messenger of hope and inspiration to all people, but especially those with disabilities and particularly those who lack limbs. When I was born, my parents were grief- and terror-stricken. They had no clue whether I could ever have a normal life. In fact, they were almost certain that they would have to take care of me for the rest of their lives.

They could see no other way because they had never seen someone like me. In my travels around the world, I've so far met twenty-four men, women, and children born with the same or a very similar body. I've also met many military veterans and accident victims who've lost all or most of their limbs. Few things give me more joy than being able to comfort them and offer them hope that it is possible for them to lead a meaningful and fulfilling life.

If my parents had found someone who had raised a child like me, someone to help and guide them, their grief and fear would have been diminished significantly. If I'd had another person like me to serve as a role model, my life would have been much easier. When people ask me if I was worried that my son could have been born without limbs, my answer is that as long as my son loves God, that is all he will need. I would rather see him have a life without limbs than a life without God.

Many, many children come into this world with physical and mental disabilities and health challenges. I don't pretend to know what God's plan is for each and every one of them, but I do know that all of them have value and purpose. Is it scary to become a parent? Yes. Is it even scarier to become a parent of a disabled child or a child with health issues? Most certainly. Yet there are also many blessings to be discovered. My parents, who may one day write their own book on the challenges and joys of raising a disabled child, struggled mightily at first. They would also tell you that dealing with my disabilities drew them closer to God and expanded their faith.

If you are the parent of such a child, or if you were born with challenges yourself, I am here to encourage and support you. More importantly, you have the most powerful ally in our Father in heaven. I also want to reach out to those who are struggling or have struggled to conceive a child. While modern medical science can help overcome many of the obstacles to conception, I know there are some who have not yet received the miracle of a child. I encourage you and support you in your efforts.

In recent years I've met a number of married couples who received their miracle gift from God through adoption. My friends Andie and Lee Hendrickson of Phoenix have inspired me with their efforts to adopt and care for three children with special needs or the potential for special needs. I've visited many orphanages and foster care facilities around the world, of course, but the Hendricksons have made me even more aware of the need for loving, caring, and faith-filled adoptive parents.

There are hundreds of thousands of kids in orphanages and foster homes. I've seen the healing and restoration and transformation that adoptive parents can bring to these children, many of whom had felt abandoned and unloved. My friends who've adopted children say that their lives are also changed by opening their heart and home to those who otherwise might never have a foundation of trust and stability.

Loving and caring adoptive and foster parents are heroes in my mind. They trust that God's perfect plan will be done. They know that all children are children of God. I encourage all couples to be open to adoption or foster parenting. I can't imagine the sorrow of not being able to have your own child, but I have witnessed the joy of those called by God to step up and be a miracle for a child who so badly needs one.

Every life is a gift. Every moment of life is yours to treasure. Suffering is part of life, but joy is available in abundance as well. If you look for the joy, you will find it and then it will find you and help ease your suffering. I have known the darkness. I fight it off nearly every day through prayer and by accepting the love around me. If I can help you in any way, I am here. In fact, I believe it is why I am here.

Expecting a Blessing

During Kanae's pregnancy, some encouraged us to do genetic testing on our baby, but we felt that no matter what the results were, it would not change anything. We wanted this child. We knew God wanted us to have this child. Kanae wisely noted that many tests give off false positives, so why do tests that could cause her to stress out during the pregnancy for no reason. This is a very personal decision, of course. If you think there is a reason to do more testing on your child, that is your choice. Our only advice is to educate yourself by reading and talking to more experienced mothers about all aspects of pregnancy, including the tests that are mandatory and those that are optional.

If you have medical professionals in the family, I recommend you use them as a resource too. Most will be glad to offer their guidance. My mother was an incredible resource for us, because she had served for years as a midwife and also because she learned a great deal in having three children of her own— especially me, the challenging child.

Because it's easy to get stressed out during pregnancy with all of the hormones flowing in your body, Kanae says that expectant mothers should be careful as they educate themselves on pregnancy.

〜〜〜

You should learn as much as you can, but know, too, that many websites, books, and articles focus a lot on what can go wrong simply because they want to cover all of the possibilities. There is a risk that reading about all the things that can go wrong will freak you out and make you think that every little kick or poke is the sign of something awful. So you have to understand that even if you have problems during your pregnancy, your doctor will likely be able to control them and guide you to a successful delivery. I know it's easy to say "Don't worry," but it's a lot more difficult to have faith that your baby will be okay. That's one reason it was so helpful for me to have Nick's mom, Dushka, and his sister, Michelle, who is also a nurse, to talk to whenever I had concerns. They were very good at reassuring me and easing any fears that I had.

〜〜〜

Our goal during Kanae's pregnancy was to do no more than necessary in order to reduce stress on Kanae and the baby, and me, too! (I'm still the challenging child in many ways.) We did agree to go to a high-risk pregnancy clinic just to make sure the baby was developing properly. Given my parents' experience with me, we also consented to more ultrasound tests, including some in 3-D. They all looked fine, and Kanae joked that she could make a whole baby album just out of the ultrasounds.

Even after Kanae had all the checkups required for a new mother and everything looked fine, we were reluctant to tell anyone outside our immediate family. Most doctors advise you to get through the first thirteen weeks before making such announcements, because after that the chance of a miscarriage diminishes significantly, especially for healthy young women like Kanae.

We were just overly excited. We did share the awesome news. And let's just say…I think really exciting news spreads faster than bad news.

As you get older you realize that it is important for family members to keep secrets for each other, because you can't possibly know all of the implications of revealing them. Kanae and I understood why everyone was so excited and happy for us. Our child was to be the first grandchild on both sides. We are grateful for their love. In this case, everything worked out just fine, and of course we are grateful for that as well.

Our advice to other couples expecting their first child is to be very careful about sharing the information, because it's almost impossible to limit where it spreads. This is a very personal decision, of course, and we are well aware of the temptation to shout your joy from the rooftops. We've read and heard many stories of couples who've had a tough time during pregnancies, so we're aware and thankful that our first experience was such a glorious one.

I didn't think I could love my wife more than I loved her on our wedding day, but every day of her pregnancy seemed to draw us closer together. It was such an amazing experience. When Kanae had her first ultrasound, it was like a party broke out in the examining room, we were so elated.

I was expecting to see just a tiny unrecognizable figure, almost like a little black dot, and then when the moment came, and I saw our baby on the screen, he was so beautiful! I could see this little person's head with little arms and little legs. I had a couple of tears and so did Nick, and we were so happy, we were actually laughing ecstatically. I forgot all about everything else going on. Nick's mom was there, and she was taking cell phone pictures of the screen and laughing with us.

⌒ᴗⲐⲐⲐ

Apart from the ultrasounds, we didn't do any testing that was suggested for other types of disabilities our son might have. We would have accepted him just the way he was, no matter what. We had no concerns that our baby would lack limbs, but I will admit that we were both excited and relieved when we saw his fingers and toes on the screen. It was an unbelievably joyful moment. When the technicians took their measurements of the head and body, they gave us their estimated delivery date of February 12—the first anniversary of our wedding! How crazy was that?

It seemed so surreal because things were moving so quickly. The reality really sank in at that point. And so did the fact that I was booked to do a scattered four-month world tour immediately after our child was to be born.

Baby Timing

For all of the joy that we felt with our baby news, Kanae and I quickly realized that we were about to dive into parenthood with little preparation and only a few months of experience as husband and wife. There was also the fact that we'd planned on seeing the world together on my twenty-four-country speaking tour in Southeast Asia and Latin America, as well as Kanae's native Mexico.

So we could have been tempted to say that the timing wasn't great for starting a family. But we rejected that thought for many reasons. We saw this child as a blessing, particularly since we knew other couples who had been trying for years to have a child. Wanting a child and not being able to conceive is one of the most wrenching experiences any couple can have, so we certainly were not about to gripe that the timing wasn't perfect. We were grateful beyond measure.

I've had more experienced fathers tell me that you can always find a reason that the timing to have a child isn't perfect. It's a life-changing, highly disruptive, chaotic, financially challenging, health-endangering, patience-trying, and relationship-testing experience. Think about it: A whole new person is joining you and your spouse. That little person will cry loudly, disrupt your sleep, constantly have needs to be met, and want to be the center of attention. You will have to feed, clothe, and care for that person, and that person is not going away for a long, long time. Eighteen years, at least!

When is there a good time for that?

I'm making a joke, of course, but also a point. You can argue that there is no such thing as a perfect time to have a child. I will turn that argument around and say that any time is the perfect time for a married couple to have a child. You say you don't have a big enough home? enough money in the bank? the time to take off your job? a stroller? a baby crib?

Certainly I encourage you to have a solid financial foundation and a safe place to raise your child, but you need to have a little faith too. You can't wait for the "perfect" time because it may never come. Like most first-time parents, Kanae and I were about as unprepared as any couple could be, but once we found out she was pregnant, we embraced parenthood and committed to doing the best we could. With God's strength and guidance, we prepared ourselves for this gift. You will figure it out too.

Preparing for an unplanned child can be scary and intimidating. Yet there are many people—couples and single parents as well—who pull it off with fewer resources and less support than we had. You may have to make sacrifices, abandon or adjust your plans, trade the sports car for an SUV, and turn your man cave into a baby's bedroom, but you can do it, I promise.

Kanae and I had many adjustments to make. Some of them we resisted at first. For a very brief moment, we thought she and the baby could accompany me on the world tour. We even purchased a traveling baby crib, an infant car seat that could be used on airplanes, and other devices and gear, but we quickly realized the stress and strain would be too great for both Kanae and the baby.

We prayed together, hoping that I could cancel the tour even though contracts had been signed, venues rented, tickets sold, and commitments made. But many people were counting on me to make the appearances. So I had to man up and accept that for the first critical months of our child's life, I would be there in person only intermittently, or communicating by phone, Skype, or FaceTime.

My sacrifice would be nothing like the challenges faced by Kanae, and we both knew that. We did our best to prepare for it, and then we prayed that God would provide what we could not. He certainly provided her with an easy pregnancy in terms of how she felt. Of course that's easy for me to say since my body wasn't undergoing a radical transformation, but she mostly agrees, believe it or not.

∻

I had such a cool pregnancy and felt great the whole time. But one thing I wish I had done was take more time to relax and meditate and just pamper myself during pregnancy. I cherished the time that Nick and I had as a married couple before the baby came. Ideally, we might have liked to have had the two years we originally planned just to ourselves, but God had other things in mind for us, and I certainly am grateful for the gift of our child. Still, I didn't give a lot of thought to the fact that my pregnancy would be the last time for many years when I could have myself to myself. Does that make sense?

Again, I would not change a thing about becoming pregnant when it happened, but to other women, I might say that if you are in a similar situation and have no children, I would encourage you to take some time each day, or at least once a week, to savor your downtime. Appreciate those moments you might be able to claim as your own so that you can relax in the bathtub or shower or on the beach or with a good book or favorite movie.

I say that because you won't have much opportunity to pamper yourself or savor downtime once you have a baby. In truth, I was very grateful to have an infant to pamper when ours arrived. My mothering instincts kicked in, and my focus shifted entirely to caring for my child. It was a very natural transition. But I would recommend that you enjoy your quiet time while you can, because there won't be as many opportunities to do that once your child arrives.

I was also very fortunate to have no bouts of morning sickness. My energy levels were higher than ever before. I love to work in the garden and so does Nick's mom, Dushka. So, one day during my pregnancy, we were out working alongside the landscapers, putting in our plantings. Nick and the other boys were being very protective, saying I shouldn't be on my knees digging holes and planting, but Dushka stood up for me. 'If she feels like she can do it, let her do it!' She told me not to let them coddle me because pregnant women are much hardier than people realize. Women rock! So if you want to be active and your doctor hasn't given you any restrictions, go for it!

The first six or seven months, the doctor thought I wasn't gaining enough weight and I was a little low on iron, but honestly, I never even felt like taking a nap. I never had adverse reactions to certain tastes or smells that many pregnant women experience, nor did I have any cravings.

But my husband did! Isn't that right, Nick?

It's true, I confess! Late in Kanae's pregnancy, I began to have these overpowering cravings for milk with my beloved chocolate Tim Tams, a layered malted biscuit. I used to gobble these up as a child in Australia, but for some reason, as an adult I decided that the ultimate Tim Tam experience was to bite off both ends and then suck milk through it like a straw! The really odd thing was that while I had always been a Tim Tam fanatic, I never liked milk until Kanae became pregnant. I found myself craving milk even when there were no Tim Tams around. In fact, I still drink cold milk today, especially before I go to bed. Strange, but true!

Twelve

Our Little Explosion of Hope

ince Kanae did all of the work in the delivery room, we thought she should tell this part of our story, so here she is.

❧

February 12, 2013, arrived—our first wedding anniversary and the baby's due date. Our parents, my sister, and my grandmother had all come in anticipation of the delivery, but apparently the baby hadn't gotten the memo. Other than some slight cramps and a few minor contractions, I felt fine.

I went to my doctor's appointment that day as scheduled. She and I were both surprised that I was dilated four centimeters, which is generally considered to mark the progression from the first to the second stage of the three-stage birthing process. Since I wasn't having any pain, my doctor gave me the choice of going to the hospital or just going home and resting. I was afraid that if I went to the hospital, they might induce labor with medication. We wanted to keep this as natural as possible, so I went home.

I walked in the door and was greeted by a huge flower arrangement Nick had ordered to celebrate our first anniversary. We had a very chill day, celebrating with family and waiting for our firstborn to arrive. Around 6 p.m., I was relaxing in the bath when the contractions began to pick up. I went to bed around

11 p.m., hoping to get another night's sleep before going to the hospital, but that wasn't going to happen. The pain was to the point where I couldn't sleep or even think about much else.

Nick's mom, the veteran delivery room nurse and midwife, was up with me, but everyone else had gone to bed. Eventually, we had to wake up Nick, my mom, Yoshie, and my grandmother because they wanted to go to the hospital with us. It was very cold, so Dushka made sure the car was warmed and the seats heated before we headed for Simi Valley Adventist Hospital about fifteen minutes away.

When the doctors checked me out at the hospital, I was still in the very early stages, so they had me do The Walk, which is familiar to many women who've had children. Wearing my hospital gown and dragging a mobile IV, I walked the hallways of the hospital from midnight until 6 a.m. Your goal is to get the baby down and in the best possible position for the delivery. The Walk is no walk in the park. Our baby was putting pressure on my lower back, causing a pain that felt like someone was holding a blowtorch to my spine.

My mom stayed with me, massaging my back. Nick was there in his electric wheelchair, and every now and then I'd rest on it, taking a break, trying to breathe, as the burning pain increased with every minute. Yoshie took all of this in and announced, "I'm never having a baby!"

I did the breathing exercises I'd learned in prenatal classes, but they didn't seem to help all that much. My family was all around, but as the time wore on, I was in too much pain to talk. I was in survival mode. I was no longer thinking about the beautiful baby on the way; I was thinking I wanted to get this over with soon.

Like many women who love the idea of natural childbirth, I'd hoped to have my baby without using painkillers, but of course I'd hoped for that before I'd been in pain. Now I was hoping for an epidural, and very soon! My advice to other pregnant women is to not try to be the hero. You will get all sorts of conflicting information about what is best. It's your decision, but you don't want to be in so much pain that you can't fully experience the joy of bringing your child into the world.

Baby Business

During my pregnancy, I watched a documentary called *The Business of Being Born* that advocates natural childbirth and even water births at home with midwives. The documentary generally put down hospitals as more about business than caring. One of the allegations was that they too often try to rush deliveries and their doctors push C-sections, because it's easier for them and carries less liability. The film took the position that hospitals are focused on making money more than on providing quality care and the best experience for patients.

There are many medical professionals who agree that high malpractice insurance fees and hospitals that put profits first have resulted in far too many C-sections and increased the cost of having a baby. Most advise you to choose your doctor and your hospital carefully. Talk to friends and family members about their experiences. It's your choice, whether you want to go to a hospital or deliver your child at home. Most doctors will tell you, however, that if something goes wrong during a delivery, you may need the sort of rapid emergency treatment and professional care that you won't likely get at home.

In the Delivery Room

My experience with doctors and hospitals during my pregnancy with our first child was marked by both good and bad moments. I did sometimes feel like my physician was in a rush, yet most of my nurses were wonderful and very empathetic and attentive. Then again, I've always tried to avoid the medical system if I could. I don't even like taking aspirin for a headache unless it's so painful I can't deal with it.

As the baby begins to move into birth position, you quickly learn the limits of your ability to endure pain. Everyone is different, of course, but my plans quickly changed as the birthing process began. Some say an epidural can make the birth more difficult because it can decrease your ability to push, but in the end I decided that if God has provided medicine that can ease the pain, I would not turn it down if I needed it.

Unfortunately, my anesthesiologist was at home and had to drive forty-five minutes to get to the hospital. If I could have sent the medical helicopter for him, I would have. I didn't cry until he walked in the door; by that time, I was in so much pain the thought of finding relief brought me to tears. As soon as they put the needle in my back, the baby moved, and between that shift in position and the epidural drugs, I felt so much better. I actually slept for a couple of hours with Nick at my side, and when I woke up around 8 a.m., the baby was ready to come.

Once my water broke, they took me into the delivery area waiting room. The nurses had me do the pushing exercises for forty-five minutes while we waited for my doctor to finish with another patient. The nurses were wonderful, giving me massages with oils. When my doctor arrived, we talked again about the fact that I wanted the baby to be put on my tummy right after birth. I'd read that there were benefits to doing that, and I liked the idea, but as it turned out, that didn't go according to plan.

Things then moved quickly, and to be honest, I probably wouldn't have so many people in my room the next time because it was painful. Our baby was bigger than the doctors had thought he'd be, and he was having trouble getting out. My family members wanted to be there for me, but I think having my husband there will be enough for me next time. Kiyoshi, though, was the first grandchild on both sides, so it was very special for everyone.

It was also very emotional, and by the time our baby came out, it was hard to tell who was crying the loudest, my husband or my grandmother.

Actually, Nick was much quieter than my grandmother. He had a few tears though, and then there was this very beautiful moment. Right after delivery, the doctor cradled our son in her arms and said, "Wow, he is a giant!" Just then, the baby opened his eyes and turned to Nick, and they just looked at each other with such love!

I'll let Nick tell you what that felt like.

I had often thought of what it would be like to see my child for the first time, and I can tell you now that it was absolutely incredible. When Kanae was giving birth, we were all so excited but also concerned for her and the baby at the same time. When we could see the baby's head and shoulders, everyone became so joyful. I had tears streaming down my face as he came all the way out, and the doctor dealt with the umbilical cord while she held him on her arm.

I'd been told that normally a newborn can't see more than a foot in front of his face, but I was about twice that distance from our son when he first opened the bluest eyes I'd ever seen and looked right at me. Everyone was saying, "He's looking at Daddy!"

I thought, *Oh, my gosh, he's looking into my soul.* I was breathless. Time seemed to stop while we looked at each other with such intensity. It was an experience beyond compare, a miracle. Then the nurse took him to weigh him and clean him up, and it seemed so long before they finally brought him back and gave him to Kanae to nurse.

When my dad held our son, his first grandchild, it was another special moment. I've never seen him so happy. He seems to be at a new level of joy ever since becoming a grandfather. It's wonderful to see that, almost as good as becoming a father myself!

Okay, back to Kanae.

The nurses took Kiyoshi to be cleaned, weighed, and measured (8 lbs., 10 oz., 21.75 in. long), and it seemed like they were gone with him forever! Because Kiyoshi's bigger shoulders got stuck for a bit, they wanted to take that extra time to make sure he was okay. That extra time bothered me because I wanted to bond with him on my tummy right away. It was so funny, though. When they did bring him back, he was naked and so pink and cute, with perfect skin tone. He was beautiful!

Right away everyone tried to figure out who he looked like, which was very funny and a true challenge because of his unique blend of Japanese, Mexican, and Serbian heritage. Our family decided he had my Asian eyes, with Nick's chin and ears. I guess you could say he looks like 25 percent Japanese, 25 percent Mexican, and 50 percent Serbian, so far, but you know how children can change as they grow older. When he was born his eyes were very blue, but now they are becoming darker and darker brown.

Our son will not only have very interesting looks given his mixed heritage, but the Japanese Serbian name we gave him will reflect it as well. His first name is Kiyoshi, which was my father's name. Nick loved the idea of giving our baby my father's name, which made me very happy. It was a special moment when I called my father's mother—my grandmother—in Shizuoka, Japan, and told her. She thanked and thanked me. She was so happy she cried.

Kiyoshi's name is also especially appropriate because we'd heard that it means "explosion of hope." Of course, since our son's birth, we've heard several other interpretations from Japanese friends, and we love them all, including "innocent soul," "accessing heaven," and "beautiful tree."

Postpartum Is No Party

One thing I would advise a mom-to-be is to research what life is like immediately after you deliver your baby into the world. Many tend to focus so much on pregnancy and delivery that they don't take the time to prepare for those sometimes challenging days that follow the arrival of a child.

I wanted to think that the joy of having our child would lift my spirits so much that the recovery period would be a breeze. It wasn't, I'm sorry to say. My recovery was not exceptionally difficult compared to most mothers, but then most mothers will tell you that postpartum is harder than they'd imagined it would be.

I wasn't prepared for the fact that you can't even sit down for the first week because of the stitches and other challenges that are part of the typical postpartum package. I was grateful to have my mother and mother-in-law around to help me. My mom stayed for four days. But even with their support, it was a very difficult time. My advice is to forget about being Supermom and ask for as much help as you can round up for the first week or two after coming home from the hospital.

Sore and Sad

After the joyous high of delivery and seeing your newborn, mothers may well experience the sad lows of postpartum—both emotionally and physically. It's all part of the good news–bad news of parenting, I guess. Part of me would just as soon not even mention it, because I don't want to be a kill-joy for any expectant mom. Still, I think it's better to help prepare you for what can be a difficult and disorienting time. I have to plead guilty to skipping over the bad news section in all of my prenatal reading just because I didn't want to think about postpartum pain and anguish. Of course, then I was surprised at just how hard it hit me!

Your own experience may be vastly different from mine, depending on whether you have a vaginal or Caesarean delivery, normal or complicated. I had only some minor complications during my vaginal delivery, but even they were more scary and painful than I'd anticipated. The postpartum days were definitely not fun for me, nor are they for most moms.

Having a baby may be a natural thing, but our body goes through incredible stress and wear and tear in the process. Then, in the days after delivery, doctors say we can look forward to the further insult of bleeding, cramps, sweats, constipation, hemorrhoids, fatigue, backaches, breast pain and leaks, not to mention all of the lingering pain from areas damaged during delivery.

New moms should be prepared for dealing with a very sore body, very little sleep, and a very needy baby. There is nothing low maintenance about a new-born. I chose to breast-feed, which also can be painful and accompanied by cramping. Despite the joys of being a new mother, there were times when I wondered, *When will this be over?*

I thought I would never catch up on my sleep. I had heard about the "baby blues," but I had such an easy pregnancy I convinced myself that they wouldn't happen to me. No such luck! I've never been a crybaby, but my baby made me one. For about four or five days, I was like an exposed nerve. Little things that really were not important hit me ten times harder because of all my raging hormones.

I nearly snapped off Nick's head when he tried to share with me something we'd learned in neonatal classes about positioning the baby for breast-feeding! Poor guy, he was just trying to help. I think I scared him! He's not used to Crazy Kanae. Fortunately, he knew it was the postpartum hormones going crazy, not me.

Your hormone levels dive after giving birth, which creates sharp mood swings and the sense that you will never get your normal life and body back. With the blues on top of all the pain and discomfort and lack of sleep, it's amazing we get through those first few weeks.

Like a lot of new moms, I had to give myself a break and take the long view in order to survive. It helped to remind myself that this wasn't the way it would always be. One friend said when she got the blues and cried her husband told her to just tell herself that it was like watching a sad movie produced and directed not by the Coen Brothers but the Hormone Sisters—Estrogen and Progesterone.

I like that idea! It did help for me to try and separate myself from the dark moods and sadness. I'd remind myself that it happens to most new mothers and it is a small price to pay for our beautiful baby boy. Like many young mothers, I was used to doing anything I wanted before the baby. We were remodeling the house and putting in a garden, and I wanted to help. But a hungry newborn does not understand when his mother has other things to do.

My advice is to go easy on yourself. Focus on the baby and don't worry about making yourself or your home or yard perfect, or even close to what they would normally be. I was fortunate that I wasn't working outside the home or going to school when the baby arrived. I'm sure the pressure would have been even greater to bounce back if I'd had a job or studies. Women are so hard on them-selves, and they rarely cut themselves a break, but if you've just had a baby, now is the time to do that.

I don't like to be a burden to anyone, but again this is the time to get help if you can. It doesn't help the baby if mom is exhausted. Once my mother left, I knew I could call on Nick's mother to help if I needed her. I still tried to do too much on my own. And I encourage other new mothers to call all helping hands on deck.

It helped to pamper myself a little while the baby slept by taking a nap, showering, or catching up on e-mails and Facebook. Mothers in the postpar-tum period have to take their pleasures where they can get them. Even just walking around our yard in the sunshine was a welcome relief. I'm not a big eater, so I also had to be careful to keep snacking and eat regular meals, be-cause it's easy for a new mom to zap her energy and blood sugar levels, espe-cially if she is breast-feeding.

Like many expectant and new moms, I fell into the Supermom trap of want-ing to do everything perfectly. Since we live in California, I was exposed to all the latest, trendy green and high-tech baby goodies. I wanted to have as natural a childbirth as I could manage—safely, of course. And then there is all the pressure to use organic diapers and environmentally friendly strollers, baby seats, and on and on.

You reach a point where you just have to go with common sense and your maternal instincts. At least I did. Trying to be the perfect mom only adds to the stress at a time when your defenses are down anyway. I decided simply to focus on keeping my baby fed, safe, and as happy as possible, while doing the same for Nick and myself.

Baby Bonding

One of the greatest joys in the hospital and then at home for the first few days was watching our son bond with his proud daddy. Right after Kiyoshi was born and we were in my hospital room, Nick would lie down beside me and have me put Kiyoshi on his chest. Nick's heartbeat is faster than that of most people, and without limbs to let off body heat, he stays warm all the time. Kiyoshi seemed to love the warmth of resting on Nick's chest.

Nick loved it so much he didn't want to give up Kiyoshi, even when the nurses came to give him his bath. He became very protective too, not wanting Kiyoshi to get his first vaccine shots because he didn't want our boy to feel pain so soon after birth. I had to overrule him there, playing the "mother knows best" card.

When Nick is home, he tends to be very restless and active, bouncing all over the house as he talks business on his phone headset or having Skype meetings on his laptop. He's always busy setting up speaking engagements, talking with his staff and advisors, and exploring new opportunities and projects. That changed when Kiyoshi joined us. Nick was scheduled to hit the road for a world tour, so he wanted to get in as much time with Kiyoshi and me before he left. It was so sweet to watch my boys bond.

Newborn Challenges

As wonderful as it was to have our baby home with us, and as grateful as we were for him, there were challenges in those first few weeks. At times it was really stressful. I want to be truthful with you so if you are just starting a family you can be prepared and, hopefully, take some steps to make sure you have all the information, help, and support you need. I decided to breast-feed Kiyoshi, because I believed that was the best way to nurture him. Breast-feeding has many benefits for the baby, but it is not the easiest thing in the world for the mother.

I became a little overwhelmed, in part because I was so worn out and still in pain from the delivery. I didn't have time to read the instructions for the breast pump thoroughly, and as a result, my breasts became engorged, which was very painful. Kiyoshi was also feeding for an hour and a half each time, and I couldn't tell if he was just using me as a pacifier or actually getting the nourishment he needed, so that was a challenge too.

The most difficult thing, though, was when he got colic that lasted three months. It was a very stressful time, because he would cry and cry and cry at night, and it seemed like there was nothing we could do to quiet him. The first time this happened, Kiyoshi was only four weeks old. We went with Nick on a business trip to Oregon, and none of us could sleep in our hotel room. Nick had been speaking and making appearances all day, and he and I were both exhausted. This was the first time I felt truly helpless, because it seemed like there was nothing I could do.

I had heard of colic, but I really didn't understand what it was or how to deal with it. As it turns out, nobody really understands what causes it, and apparently it isn't something that does the baby much harm. Most of the people I've talked to and the things I've read say it is harder on the parents than the baby, and I can vouch for that.

Kiyoshi's case was pretty much in line with what I've been able to learn about it. Only about 20 percent of newborns between the ages of three weeks and three months get it. Kiyoshi would start crying in the afternoon or at night and wail and wail for two or three hours, almost screaming. His face would turn really red, and he'd kick and claw like he was in great pain. It was awful!

Most pediatricians recommend that you bring in a baby who has extended bouts of crying and screaming. It may just be colic, but you want to be sure it isn't something else, like an infection, an intestinal or kidney blockage, or something else you can't easily detect yourself.

I've heard theories that colic is caused by stomach gas, overstimulation, acid reflux, and lactose intolerance. Some mothers who bottle-feed say it sometimes helps to change from a milk-based formula to a soy-based formula, but I was breast-feeding, so that wasn't an option. Other sources suggest breast-feeding moms try eliminating certain things from their diet, one by one, to see if it helps reduce colic. These include cabbage, milk, caffeine, onions, chocolate, and garlic.

I've also heard all sorts of ways to try and soothe colicky babies. Some sources say motion can be helpful. One father said he would put their colicky and wailing infant son in the stroller, listen to music cranked up on his headphones, and push the baby stroller around the dining room table until either the baby stopped crying or the dad collapsed from exhaustion.

I've heard other moms say they'd put their babies in car seats and take them for a drive when they were having colic attacks, but I'm not sure driving with a screaming baby in the backseat is a good idea. Another mom told me that she would put the car seat, with her baby securely buckled in, on top of the clothes dryer. When she turned on the dryer, the vibration and noise would calm the baby. Please note that she put the baby in the car seat *on top of* the dryer—*not in* the dryer!

White noise is also helpful. I've heard of moms trying to counter the baby's crying and soothe the child by running a vacuum cleaner, hair dryer, or white noise machine, or playing soothing music.

Still others say wrapping colicky babies up in a blanket can help, but you have to make sure they don't get too hot.

The strangest thing was that Kiyoshi would cry and cry for hours at full volume, and then all of a sudden he would just stop, like there had been nothing wrong. This is the way colic usually works, but it just seemed so odd that one minute he'd be screaming like someone was sticking him with a needle, and the next he was perfectly calm.

Meanwhile, I would be like a zombie from stress and lack of sleep. I have been through very stressful situations from a young age. I lost my dad, had to run the family business, and took care of my younger brother, so I thought I could handle almost anything. But when Kiyoshi had colic, it was one of the hardest things I've ever gone through. It wore out my body, mind, and soul. You get to the point where you just want to run and find some peace somewhere, because your baby is crying and crying and you can't help him. You can't reason with a baby or ask him to tell you what is wrong. All of my maternal instincts were telling me to do something for my poor, distressed child, but nothing seemed to work.

It helps to keep in mind that most episodes last only a few hours and that babies always grow out of it eventually. Okay, so knowing that doesn't help all that much when it's 3 a.m. and you are exhausted and your husband can't stand the crying either. You are both about ready to run out of the door and dive into the deepest hole you can find. But I want to give you hope that this will not last forever.

About all you can do is try to catch up on your sleep when the baby is snoozing so you are better equipped to handle a crying baby. You may have to let the housework or your job wait, because without sleep, you really can't function very well as a mom, wife, housekeeper, or employee. You may also need to hire a very patient and experienced baby-sitter so you can get out of the house now and then to recharge, air out your brain, and relax with friends, doing something like a normal person instead of like an exhausted mom.

I've known couples who've had serious conflicts over a colicky baby. The stress levels can make your life very difficult, so you should do anything you can to give each other a break. Colicky babies seem to have been a problem since the days humans started making babies, but once again, that probably won't give you much peace.

One of my challenges was that Nick was often traveling in our baby's first six months, and we had moved to a new area, so I didn't know a lot of other young moms. I would recommend joining a neighborhood group or asking your pediatrician if there are any mother's groups or baby play groups you could join. I'm not saying misery loves company, because most of being a new mother is wonderful. But it can help to talk to other mothers who've dealt with colic. If nothing else, you can share war stories, console each other, and start a colicky baby survivor's group.

The Good Outweighs the Bad

I hope those "war stories" don't scare you if you are just starting a family. Our son, like most others, eventually stopped having his colicky bouts, and Nick and I really learned to appreciate how wonderful it is to have a quiet, happy baby again. In some ways, you could say that dealing with colic helps prepare parents for those many other times to come when circumstances beyond your control will tax your patience and strength. Feeling overwhelmed and stressed can be part of parenting, but thankfully, the good times far outweigh the bad.

We've had so many joyful moments with our son. Life just seems richer and our relationship is so much deeper now that we have him to love, hold, and raise together. You really do learn the true meaning of patience and unconditional love once you have a child, and I think we've become more patient and loving of each other as a result.

Of all the touching stories Nick tells in his speeches and videos, one of the most heartbreaking for me is when he talks about his fears as a child and young man that no woman would ever love him because he didn't have arms to hold her or a baby. It's never bothered me that he couldn't hug me the "normal" way, because he is so good at hugging the Nick way. Still, when I became pregnant, he talked about his concerns that he couldn't hold the baby like most fathers. I could tell he was fretting about it.

You can imagine my delight when his parents found a baby sling that Nick could wear around his shoulders. When Kiyoshi was very little, we could put the sling on Nick and then slip our baby into it. We started doing that when Kiyoshi was just nine days old. At first Nick was concerned that our big baby would fall or the sling would give way, but it worked out very well for a time.

Watching Nick holding Kiyoshi so close and seeing them feel each other's heartbeats and laughing and smiling at each other has been one of the greatest experiences. It makes me feel so proud that I provided my husband with such joy in our child, and that I provided our child with such a good father. Maybe the best time of all for me as a mother was when Nick was holding Kiyoshi in the sling and he looked at me and said, "I can't believe I'm a father. Holding him like this is a dream come true. I can't imagine my life without the two of you now."

Motherhood can be challenging, but the rewards, like those words from my dear husband, make it all worthwhile.

Thirteen

The Family Plan

*E*arly in the first chapter, I told you about being overwhelmed with love for my family as I returned on my flight home in 2013. This was at the end of a four-month World Outreach speaking tour. I already described how much I missed Kanae and Kiyoshi, who'd been born shortly before I'd had to leave on the tour that was scheduled before we knew Kanae was pregnant.

Initially, I'd hoped to break up the tour with a couple of extended visits home, but that had not worked out. I'd only been able to grab brief visits home with my wife and newborn son during that period. Other than that, I had visited with them only on the telephone or via Skype.

I'd spoken to millions of people live and on television during that tour. I'd also endured a terrible fever and long bouts of loneliness. I missed my family terribly. So on that return flight home, I was overjoyed at the thought of reuniting with them. I'd also felt guilty for leaving Kanae and our son so early in his life, especially since Kanae was still recovering from childbirth and coping with being a mother for the first time.

All of those emotions struck me on the flight home and left me quietly sobbing in my seat, hoping no one would notice. I had visions of coming in the front door, hugging my son, and collapsing into the loving arms of my wife. The World Outreach Tour had been amazingly successful and incredibly rewarding, but I was exhausted and in deep need of a break.

What I had not taken into consideration was that Kanae was also exhausted and in great need of a break. While I missed my wife and son, I'd also missed the first few months of what is often a very challenging time even when both spouses are present—the transition that occurs when a newborn, especially a couple's first child, is brought home.

Kanae and I thought we were well prepared for Kiyoshi's arrival in our life and in our home. We created a baby's room with a crib, changing table, dresser, baby monitor, and all of the other newborn furnishings. We were not prepared, however, for the dramatic changes our son would bring in our household, our daily life, and our relationship.

I knew there would be an increased workload for her, of course, and I felt terrible about leaving on the world tour so soon after his birth. Yet I had no idea that such a tiny person could create so much stress and even chaos.

If you already have children, you are probably shaking your head at my naiveté. But I think you have to live through this experience to truly grasp how greatly life changes and marital tensions increase when the first child comes home.

Kanae and I are not all that unique in the fact that we had a very short time to experience being husband and wife before Kiyoshi arrived. Then, we had to make another major lifestyle change as we became a family.

Neither of us had any idea of the time it takes to properly care for an infant or how all-consuming it can be, even with a healthy child. The lack of sleep, especially during Kiyoshi's colicky phase, was a major problem whenever I was home and, of course, for Kanae too. We both felt the weight of additional responsibility, including financial pressures.

During our courtship and early marriage, we had very few serious conflicts or misunderstandings, but that also changed as we felt the stress of parenthood and all the other changes, not to mention adjustments in our sex life.

My absence during the first several months of Kiyoshi's life threw us off, but the sense of being disconnected was also caused by the new pressures of parenting and the reduction in the time we had to talk and share our thoughts with each other. There is simply less freedom to do what you want to do when you are a parent. The baby's needs and comfort are always the primary concern. I read somewhere that your free time to bond as a couple is cut by a third when you become parents. That seems like a conservative estimate to me.

Unfortunately, Kanae went through the first several weeks of this experience without me, and that only added to the strain because while I was not clueless to her situation, I did not have a full understanding of it until I returned home.

When I came through the front door with my bags that night, my wife welcomed me and comforted me, but she was also looking for me to comfort her because, from her perspective, my trip was a breeze compared to what she had been dealing with.

Funny how that works isn't it?

Well, maybe not funny, but certainly enlightening!

"HONEY, I'M HOME..."

How many husbands throughout history do you think have come home from waging war, conquering enemies, sealing deals, achieving great things, and running themselves ragged, only to come through the front door and be welcomed by a wife who is every bit as worn out and ready for relief as they are?

The guy is expecting her to smother him in kisses, hand him his slippers, and lead him into the bedroom where wine glasses are on the nightstand. Instead, she unleashes her own war stories of dealing with the children and her heavy workload, then hands him a baby bottle and the diaper bag and heads out the door to hang out with her girlfriends.

That's not exactly what happened to me, of course, but I'd dare to say that the returning-warrior, worn-out-wife disconnect has occurred countless times in the history of human relationships. Some researcher will probably report one day that more of these men were wounded by their wiped-out wives than in combat.

Unlike the warriors of old, I was returning from the world of work, having survived a long stretch on the road. When I finally returned home, my goal was to hug and kiss my wife and son, then fall into bed for a couple of days with them snuggling next to me.

My wife's expectations were a bit different. She felt that she'd been a single parent for weeks at a time during my four-month tour. She saw me as *her* relief from caring for our newborn son and our household twenty-four hours a day, seven days a week!

Now, Kanae didn't come out and say that when I entered our home. She hugged me and kissed me for a long time, just as I'd dreamed about on the plane and for many weeks before. She even told me that she was proud of me for the sacrifices I'd made and for all of the hearts I'd touched and the souls reached during the tour.

In return, I apologized for being gone so long and told her that I didn't ever want to be apart for such an extended period. There were many other things I wanted to tell her, but it was then that I sensed there was some distance between us that had not been there before. That feeling was reinforced when she brought Kiyoshi to me and he was shy toward me, reaching back to his mother as if he didn't recognize me. Finally, he consented to be placed close to me, but then after a few minutes he wanted to go back to his mother. He was nestled into Kanae's shoulder, but then he peeked out and smiled at me, and I was overwhelmed with conflicting emotions. I was grateful to be back with my son and my wife but so, so sorry for every minute I'd been away.

Later, Kanae would talk about that moment as one in which there were many layers of emotions waiting to be explored and discussed, but we only got through the first one or two. We were both exhausted from carrying out our responsibilities without much support, because we were apart from each other so long.

Reconnecting

In some ways, I think wives go into survival mode in these situations, and I don't blame them. Their motherly instincts kick in and they take charge, and then when the husband comes home, it's difficult for them to shift gears. I get that now. I had not realized just how worn out Kanae was, in part because she is not a complainer. Kanae is a good soldier. She carries on with her duties and rarely lets on when she is feeling overwhelmed and run down.

In his speech at our wedding reception, my brother, Aaron, who helped me a lot when we were growing up, said he always knew the woman who married me would have to be Superwoman, and Kanae is indeed. She doesn't like me to say that because she is very humble, but it's true.

I failed to appreciate that she was lonely and worn out too. As a result, my homecoming was not as sweet as I'd hoped it would be. It took a couple of weeks for us to reconnect, to bond again as husband and wife and as a family.

I was sad to discover that it was taking a while for Kiyoshi to warm up to me, but then, from his perspective, I'd been gone for most of his life. That was an awful thing to think about. Even though I was his father and I was there for his birth and I'd been talking to him on Skype at every opportunity, I was little more than a stranger to my boy.

I had not realized that it is simply not enough to be the husband and the father and the provider; you have to be *present*. Now, again, I'm certainly not the first young man in a young marriage with a young child to need a kick in the pants before grasping this critical fact about the most important relationships in his life.

Whether in the movies, in literature, or in real life, how many times have you heard a man say to his wife, "I work my butt off for this family. Isn't that enough?"

The answer is always no. It's not enough.

As much as I'd like to write a chapter here titled "And They Lived Happily Ever After," I'm afraid that wouldn't be very honest or realistic. That's not to say Kanae and I aren't happily married or that the three of us are not a happy family. We are happy in every way imaginable, but we are also human—and I can be just as thickheaded as any other man when it comes to being aware of my wife's needs and serving them ahead of my own.

Partners and Parents in Training

In the Bible, married couples are encouraged to submit "to one another in the fear of God." When I was dating Kanae, I realized she is first of all my sister in Christ. As a Christian, she is the daughter of the King of kings, Lord of lords, Lord of all, and Lord of heaven, and I have to respect her in that regard first and foremost. As we grew closer, I came to believe that God had brought us together, that He wanted us to love each other in the same way that He loves us.

Now, just because I believed God put us together perfectly, it does not mean that we are perfect as individuals or perfect as a couple or perfect as parents. God's plan for us is to be together, and to do that, we have to rid ourselves of self-centeredness, self-indulgence, and self-serving tendencies. My reading of the Bible's teachings on love and marriage is that it's not about receiving love; it's about giving yourself up to love by putting your partner and your family first and foremost. It's about committing yourself to always be there for your wife or husband, to help them be their best and achieve their best.

We need to be loving, gracious, patient, caring, forgiving, empathetic, and maybe even telepathic when it comes to anticipating each other's needs and desires. I'm afraid Kanae is way ahead of me in that regard, but then she is about as perfect a person as I've ever known.

I have a long way to go to even catch up to her and no hope of surpassing her when it comes to being a loving and caring spouse. Getting married and having a child are major life-changing experiences. Becoming a family man changes your soul.

A Shift in Perspective

Why do I say that? Because your frame of reference for your entire existence is dramatically altered. I was single for the first twenty-nine years of my life. I left home at age twenty-three, so I was mostly on my own for six years. During those years I traveled the world in my work as an inspirational speaker and evangelist. My responsibilities were considerable, but I basically did what I wanted, whenever I wanted to do it, and my primary focus 24/7 was on the goals and objectives of my ministry. I believed I was doing God's work, serving His purpose for my life. I still think that's true. Yet during those ten years, I lived what was essentially a self-centered existence. And even "better," no one cared!

However, I was lonely, and more than a little heartsick too—that came with the territory. Then, when I met Kanae, I was lonely no more. My heart was filled with joy. When we married and then a few months later found out Kanae was pregnant, that joy only grew. I'm still amazed at the blessings God has granted me in my wife and son, who are everything to me. Now here's the soul-changing revelation: they are also excellent mirrors that reveal just how flawed and selfish a man I can be. At first, I didn't like that. Who would? When I came home from the world tour expecting to fall into my wife's arms and be coddled until I recovered from my odyssey, I was acting selfishly. The disappointment in my wife's eyes let me know that immediately. And then she gave my son to me, and he pulled away because he didn't recognize me (insert sad Nick face here). That, too, was a reflection of something I had never seen in myself. It wasn't a pretty sight, but I needed to see it if I was to become the husband, father, and family man I want to be.

Like many men, I had assumed that my wife and son understood the magnitude of my love for them, because I was working so hard to provide for them. But that is not enough. I don't do what I do for money. It feels as though I hardly work because I truly love what I do. But it is dangerous to confuse being a good provider with being the selfless husband and father who expresses his love for his family.

Men are wired to provide and protect. That is what we do for our family instinctively. When we do a good job in those roles, we make the assumption that our wives and children understand it is a display of our love for them. They usually do grasp that, at least to some degree, but they generally want and need more. They want us to be present in their lives, to be involved and engaged and to understand their feelings and concerns.

THE DADDY DEAL

When I looked into that mirror provided by my wife and son, I saw my failings through their eyes and I realized that they needed more from me than I'd been giving them.

I had actually said to Kanae before Kiyoshi's birth that I had concerns that she wouldn't have as much time for me. My parents had five years together before they had kids. I was expressing a very common concern among men awaiting the arrival of their first child, but I also know that even thinking that way was a sign that I had a lot of growing up to do.

My neediness put additional pressure and stress on Kanae, which she didn't need at all. As I recall, even while she was pregnant, I expressed my fears of being less of a priority for her than our baby. That was bad. I needed to pray for more patience and understanding.

Kanae and I are grateful to have our faith as a common bond and as the ultimate source of strength for these challenges. There are many good marriages in which God is not as present as He is in our relationship. All I can say is that our marriage is far better than it might be thanks to our prayers offered and answered, as well as the fact that God heard the prayers of hundreds who prayed for us each day.

In the next chapter, we offer you some of the insights we have gained in our admittedly limited experience as first-time parents.

Fourteen

Kanae and Me, and Kiyoshi Makes Three

*A*fter Kanae and I married, we had just a few months of learning to "become one" before we discovered we were about to become three. The training wheels were still on our marriage at that point. We were hanging in the honeymoon stage and never imagined how quickly the next nine months would fly by.

It seemed we were newlyweds one minute and parents the next. Somehow our lives were put on speed dial. Kanae and I had tried our best to prepare for the arrival of Kiyoshi, but like every other set of first-time parents, we soon discovered that you are never fully prepared for the life-altering experience of having a baby in the house.

All aspects of your life as an individual and as a couple are dramatically affected. Did you know, for example, that once you have a baby, you will never again need an alarm clock? That is because babies never sleep, or so it seems.

I wish becoming three was as easy as one, two, three, but the math is much more complicated. Kanae and I are still adjusting to being parents, but we thought it might be helpful to other young couples if we shared some of the insights and tips we've figured out so far. If you are a veteran parent, you will probably find some of this amusing, or maybe it will stir memories of your own efforts to be the first parents in history to get it right the first time.

Here then, is our...

Ten Point Survival Guide
for the First Year of Life with a Child

1. Share Your Faith

When I was a young teen and often bullied or shunned, I'd often go home and read the Bible. I found solace and even enlightenment in those readings. If you are familiar with my story, you know that it was a reading in the Bible that ended my thoughts of suicide and put me on course for the ridiculously good life I'm enjoying.

I grew up in a Christian family, but it wasn't until I was age fifteen that I gave my life to Jesus Christ, after reading from John 9. The scripture tells of Jesus meeting a villager who'd been blind since birth. A crowd was following Jesus, and one of them asked why the man was born that way.

Jesus said he was blind at birth so that "the works of God should be revealed in him." When I read that passage, I felt an incredible sense of peace, something I'd never felt before. I believe God breathed life and faith into me. It seemed that God led me to read that Scripture in answer to the question I'd long been asking: *Why did You make me this way?* I prayed for forgiveness for my sins, turned my life into His hands, praying for arms and legs but knowing that even if they didn't miraculously appear, He would use me still in His greater plan for my life.

The Bible, then, gave me my life's purpose, so you can understand why I enjoy reading it so much. Reading Bible stories has also brought peace to our marriage and our family in ways that are nothing short of a miracle. Even before we married, Kanae and I would read the Word and pray together, and it was awesome. We'd even read scriptures over the phone and then talk about them and what they meant to us. Once we were married, we were swept up in life and the demands of work and travel, but then we realized that we needed to read the Bible together more than ever before. We were like people starving for spiritual nourishment.

Kanae and I realized early into our struggles with parenthood that our biggest asset was our shared faith. Probably the wisest and most helpful thing we have done is commit to reading Bible stories together for twenty to forty-five minutes as soon as we wake up each morning, whenever it is possible. Kiyoshi often joins us in bed as we do this, so it has become a very sweet and spiritual bonding time as well.

You may find it amusing that we've been reading from *The Child's Story Bible* by Catherine F. Vos, which Kanae discovered while reading to children she baby-sat. Mrs. Vos, the wife of a famous theologian, wrote this version to read to her grandchildren. It is a very accurate version of the Bible stories, with all the narrative and historical passages told in chronological order. The chapters are written in very entertaining ways. The stories include customs and doctrines and background information that help make it informative too. The scripture is not watered down or oversimplified; in fact, we've learned that many adults enjoy reading it, especially with their children and grandchildren. Imagine our delight when we heard that Billy Graham's wife, Ruth, used it for many years to teach Bible studies.

The first time Kanae picked up a copy of *The Child's Story Bible,* she found it so fascinating that she read it for several hours without a break. When she shared it with me, I loved it too. Seriously, I told her that I often learn more from this version of the Bible than any sermon I've ever heard.

We began reading this Bible together because we sensed that our relationship bonds were not as strong as we wanted them to be after Kiyoshi was born. Our morning sessions reading together seem to get our days off to a better start. We are often up before dawn with Kiyoshi, and reading the Bible together is so much better than getting on the laptop and reading work e-mails. When we're all together like that, it's a form of meditation. We're putting God's Word in our heart so we can apply it to our daily life. It is very cool to start the day in prayer with my wife. I feel it has helped us as a pillar of strength. Kiyoshi plays with his toys and climbs all over us. It's a beautiful thing! And it helps us start the day with a thankful heart, because we're reminded that we don't have anything without Him.

2. Be Fully Present When You Are with Your Wife and Child

This sounds a little like a Zen thing, but by "being present" I mean focusing on your loved ones whenever you are around them. I have a business and an office, but I still work at home a lot, and I'm not sure that's a good thing now that we have a child. I'm thinking that if I'm physically with my wife and son, I want to be mentally focused on them as well and not on my cell phone, checking e-mails, texting, or succumbing to all the other distractions of modern life.

Since my absence during the world tour, I have been working harder to spend extra time at home and to avoid long absences. More importantly, I want to devote lots of time and attention to my son as he grows from here on out. Kanae serves as my enforcer on this. If she thinks I'm not focusing on Kiyoshi enough when we're together, she will remind me that father-son bonds are formed in these early years. She has shown me studies that say children are more secure and self-confident if they have strong bonds with their parents.

In the flurry of daily life, we tend to forget that our children watch us even more than we watch them. We are their role models and their moral and spiritual guides. When a married couple treats each other with respect and love, their children learn by their example.

I don't want to be a helicopter dad and hover over my children. I want them to have their own experiences and use their imagination to entertain themselves. But I also think it is important to be a comforting presence, a source of encouragement, and someone they can come to whenever they want to ask a question or share a thought.

I'm trying to get wired more into the family man concept. I'm a little weird in the way I can zone out and totally shut out what is going on around me if I'm thinking about a project or an opportunity. When Kanae and I were dating and first married, I was much better at going off the grid and giving all of my attention to her.

Lately, I've been working on creating better boundaries between my work life and my family life. It's about being present-minded and engaged in every moment I am with my son and my wife. I turn off my smartphone to give my full attention to my wonderful family. I've discovered that my business actually benefits, because when I return to my office, I feel invigorated and more content due to my improved relationships.

3. Practice Gratitude

The other day I walked into the family room and saw Kanae playing and laughing with Kiyoshi, and I felt this wave of gratitude for my life with them. In the past I might not have expressed that, but now I want my wife and child to know each and every day how grateful I am to be with them.

"How did I ever get *you*?" I asked Kanae.

"No, baby," she said, "how did I get *you*?"

This must have been what Uncle Batta was talking about when he told me years ago that I needed a woman who loved me as much as I loved her. (Uncle Batta, you were right, as usual!) The thing about gratitude is that when you feel it, you should express it, whether you are grateful for something a person has done for you or you are just feeling blessed because of someone in your life. This is especially true of your wife and children.

With reciprocated love, you accept each other as you are, knowing that neither of you is perfect. We all need grace, and we all need to give grace to our partners through understanding, forgiveness, and gratitude. When Kanae and I were having a bit of a struggle after I returned from the world tour, I wanted intimacy before we had really reconnected. She had been alone most of the time with the baby and dealing with the remodeling of our home and other issues. She was feeling like a single mom, and she wanted me to recognize her feelings before picking up where we'd left off in our love life.

Being a guy, I was a little slow on the uptake. It's interesting how you can wander back to that path of selfishness. My thinking was, *I've been working so hard. I've been giving and giving, and now that I'm home, I want to receive.*

Many couples have difficulty returning to a normal sex life after the birth of a child, particularly the first child. Spontaneity is no longer an option. The lack of sleep, financial pressures, the baby's erratic schedule, and last but not least, the woman's physical recovery from childbirth are all disruptive factors in this arena. As common as those issues are, it takes patience, kindness, and consideration to overcome them in the first few months after starting a family.

After being gone so long, I hadn't taken the time to express my gratitude to her for all that she'd done while I was away. In my selfishness, I focused only on what I'd done and what I needed. It was not a proud moment for me.

The whole struggle is for the man and wife to join together, to become one as a married couple so that they are considerate and grateful for each other. Getting married is the easy part. Becoming one in your moment-to-moment, daily life is what's difficult. Before every decision you make, big or small, you have to consider the input from and the impact on the other person.

Kanae has had to deal with my many weaknesses. We all go through seasons of maturity and self-knowledge. As I've grown older, I've come to realize the need to express my gratitude more often. One of my realizations is that I never learned to say please and thank you as a child. As a disabled child, I became a little too comfortable with having people do things for me. Maybe I thought the world owed me whatever I wanted since I'd been born without arms and legs. I tended to ask for things in a straightforward manner: "Give me a glass of water."

I realized that my courtesy was lacking when I visited with the family of Daniel, a child born without arms and legs whom I've been mentoring.

Daniel's parents have worked with him to teach him to say please and thank you. I was impressed with that. Now I'm much more aware of thanking people and expressing gratitude, especially to those closest to me, because I never want to take them or their love for granted.

4. Put Your Faith in Action

We have prayed more and talked about our faith more than ever before since Kiyoshi was born, and why not ask for God's help when you need it most?

After returning home from the world tour, I struggled with being patient and understanding. Finally, I realized that if you need grace, the best thing you can do is give grace to someone.

There are many times when I simply don't know how to help Kanae with our son. In those moments when I can't take him from her or feed him for her or change his diapers or bathe him to give her a break, I become frustrated and even angry, because as a man, when my wife has a problem, I want to fix it. It hurts to face the fact that sometimes I simply can't do that. This is when I pray the most, but honestly, now I pray in steady streams all day long, no matter what I'm doing. I pray for wisdom, strength, patience, and peace. I ask God to help me make the right decisions and to be a better husband and father. I pray so much because I need God for everything. Acknowledging that is humbling in some ways, but in most ways it is empowering.

Still, humility works for me. You have to be humble enough to ask God for help, especially when you feel your emotions running away with you, old insecurities reigniting, and hurtful words forming on your lips. God can go to your heart and put out those self-destructive fires.

5. Take a Team Approach

Like many people with disabilities, I had to learn to be very straightforward in asking for help when I need it, even from total strangers. I try to be gracious about it and not ask too much of people, but at times there are certain things I just can't do for myself.

Asking for help is not a problem for me. Where I run into problems is when I go into Commander Nick mode and begin issuing orders to everyone around me. Normally I only do this in work situations, like when I'm on the road. I often have to take charge when I'm trying to get things organized for a speaking engagement. I also take on that role when my team and I arrive at airports, and I need to direct the skycaps who are trying to figure out what is checked at the ticket counter (that would be the luggage) and what is a carry-on (that would be me).

Problems arise when I have been traveling a long time and use that same command-and-control approach with my wife. I always regret when I slip into that mode, and Kanae has learned to step up and take one for the team by ordering me to stand down. But she does it in a most pleasant way. "Honey, you are being a little grumpy," she says sweetly.

What she really means is "You are not my commander in chief. You are my husband. We are a team and we are equally yoked. So play nice."

I love it! She is right, of course. Marriage and family are team sports. You need each other to survive and to keep the love alive. Team members take care of each other and look out for the welfare of everyone involved. They also divvy up responsibilities according to skill sets and capabilities. Everyone makes a contribution and everyone puts the needs of the team ahead of their own needs. Like many men, being married has taught me much about being on a team and accepting that the best way to get things done is to use the approach "We are all in this together."

6. Reframe the Situation

One of the most difficult, yet most common, lessons that a new husband and father must learn is that he now must move at a much slower pace—on family time—due to all of the additional preparation and extra gear that come with a baby. A friend of mine said that once he and his wife started having children, there was no longer any chance that they could just go somewhere on the spur of the moment. "Every time we went anywhere with the kids, it was like marshaling the troops for a major deployment," he said. "Baby stroller, toys, pacifiers, diaper bags, formula bottles, wet wipes, medications, first-aid treatments, baby food, sippy cups…after a while we could no longer fit into an SUV! We needed a Winnebago or a Mayflower moving van just to go to a soccer game."

That same friend offered this advice when he found out I was going to be a father: "Hurry up and learn patience!" I thought he was kidding. But soon I understood exactly what he meant.

Because I use a wheelchair, we already have quite a bit to pack into our SUV, but after all these years, I have a pretty good system that allows me to get moving quickly. It didn't take long to figure out that babies move at their own pace, and that between my gear and the baby support system, Kanae had her hands full anytime we all left the house, because my hands weren't available to help her.

A week or so after I returned from the World Outreach Tour, we went to Sunday church services with Kiyoshi for the first time. We had to drop Kiyoshi off in the nursery with their staff. We planned to leave the stroller there, but his diaper bag was on the stroller and Kanae had left her wallet in the diaper bag. A staff person had told Kanae she shouldn't leave any belongings on the stroller, and she seemed to be taking a long time to ponder that. Meanwhile, I was anxious to get to our seats as the worship had already started.

I suggested that she leave the diaper bag but take her wallet. My tone was less than patient, and I hurt her feelings. What I failed to understand was that there was more going on in that moment than I realized. Kanae told me later that as we were handing our son to the nursery staff, it hit her that she'd never before left Kiyoshi with a stranger and she had a minor mother freak-out: "I wasn't worried about my wallet. I was worried about leaving our son in the hands of someone I did not know."

Kanae's maternal instincts and her bond with our son are very strong. I'm grateful for that and I want to honor it. Instead of being impatient and thinking she was moving too slowly, I should have reframed this situation. Reframing really just involves a shift in perspective. It's easy to do if you are mindful of your perceptions and how they are filtered through past experiences, emotions, and thoughts.

Another friend provided me with an example of this. He came home after a hard day at work resigned to the fact that he had to mow the yard before he could relax. When he took the mower into the backyard, he discovered the yard was littered with children's toys. His kids and apparently all the others in the neighborhood had left balls, bats, tricycles, bicycles, dolls, and other playthings strewn everywhere. As he stood there surveying all the cleanup awaiting him, an older neighbor walked up and offered this perspective-shifting suggestion: "Think of it this way: before you know it, they will all be grown up and gone, and you will miss them terribly. Take it from me."

In that instant, my friend's perspective did shift. He went from being agitated about all the toys in the yard he wanted to mow to being grateful that he still had several years to enjoy having his children at home.

What a gift that neighbor gave him! My friend passed it on to me, and I should have put it to work. Instead of looking at my wife as someone who wasn't moving quickly enough, I should have looked at her as a loving mother who was reluctant to leave her son with the nursery worker because Kanae cares about him so much. The bond between a mother and her children is often beyond comprehension, even for the most understanding husband and father.

I've heard women say that when their children are hurting, they feel the pain. From what I've seen with Kanae and Kiyoshi, I believe that is possible. And I need to keep that perspective in mind.

7. Understand That You Don't Have to Fix Everything

My name is Nick and I have a confession to make: *I can't handle it when our baby cries!* Seriously, if Kiyoshi cries even remotely long, I have to leave the room or the house. If we're in the car, I have to bail out at the nearest stop. It's not something I'm proud of. Believe me, I've tried to drown out his cries with music and headphones, but nothing seems to work.

Part of the difficulty may be that I can't just go to him and pick him up, and that frustrates me and makes me aware once again of my disabilities. Like most men, when there is a problem, I want to fix it. I can't "fix" my son's crying by holding him like Kanae can.

We've also learned that there are times when you should just let your child cry until he wears himself out and goes to sleep. For instance, when Kiyoshi is supposed to be sleeping in his crib, he might cry in protest, but we've been advised that as long as we've made sure he's okay, we should leave him in the crib so he gets used to sleeping there.

Kanae can go to him and just lean over Kiyoshi and talk to him soothingly while he cries. Sometimes that works for her. It never seems to work for me—I just want him to stop. This was especially frustrating when he had colic and could cry for a couple of hours at a stretch. Of course, that was just as tough, if not more so, on Kanae.

I've had to accept that when I can't fix a situation with our son, I need to let his mother do what she does best. It's been a humbling experience, but blessed are the humble, right? I do have some male friends who say I'm lucky because I never have to pick up after my son or do the dishes. But I wish I could be of more help to Kanae around the house. Really, I do!

8. Communicate to Connect

There have been times when I've just tossed out an invitation to someone and then I'd remember to tell Kanae, usually at the last minute, "Oh, babe, we're having some people over for dinner tonight, did I tell you that? They'll be here in about a half hour." Ouch!

My wife is pretty tolerant, obviously, but after the third or fourth time she had to scramble to clean the house and prepare a meal, she reminded me that communication is better than *ex*-communication, just as a wife is better than an *ex*-wife.

When I'd invite people to our home without telling my wife, I wasn't just cutting her out of the communication loop, I was forcing her to scramble and prepare the house and the meal. I was being inconsiderate. I could hardly blame her when she said it seemed like I was treating her more like an employee than someone I loved and respected. I wasn't thinking about the extra work she had to do, and I wasn't being empathetic. It hurt her that I wasn't more considerate, and I should have been more attuned to her feelings.

I am a professional speaker. I communicate for a living. But I wasn't communicating very well with my wife when it came to my spontaneous socializations. Part of the problem is that I have so much going on that I have a tendency to put things on my calendar and then forget about them until the date comes up. So we had a family team meeting, and I agreed to put as much effort into communicating at home as I do with others around the world. One of the things we did that has been helpful is to link our online calendars so that when I make changes and additions to my schedule, Kanae is notified and she can adjust her own calendar.

My wife has also had to remind me from time to time that while I am an accomplished speaker, my listening skills are still in need of some work. Our premarital counselor made mention of this, telling us that couples should think in terms of connecting even more than communicating. That is good advice for husbands and wives, don't you think?

9. Don't Be a Bully at Home

As an anti-bullying activist, I hear bullying stories from around the world, either in conversations with members of my audience or via e-mail to my websites or Facebook page. Most people tend to think of bullying as something that goes on in schools, on playgrounds, or at the office. Yet many of the saddest and cruelest stories I've heard are about bullying that takes place in the home and within the family.

It's very sobering for me as a new husband and father to learn about the prevalence of bullying among married couples and parents and their children. I've also witnessed it in restaurants or at parties. I've seen both husbands and wives mock, criticize, and put down the other spouse in public settings. What they hope to accomplish by bullying the person they live with is beyond me. I've witnessed a husband bully his wife, and the look on her face just broke my heart. The man may have tried to make light of it or brush it off, but his wife's expression betrayed her pain. She looked as though she'd lost her best friend, which expresses very well how she feels.

We are supposed to love and praise our spouse, not bully him or her. Sometimes this begins as gentle teasing between spouses, but it can quickly turn ugly as the jabs get more and more hurtful. One wife wrote to me about her husband always putting her down because she hadn't lost weight from her pregnancy. He's even done it in front of their friends and family members. I've seen a wife do the same thing to her husband who has gained weight or fallen out of shape.

Maybe a spouse thinks they are being helpful by admonishing a spouse to lose weight, but I think it borders on cruelty and abuse. It often seems like a control issue or an example of someone trying to feel better by putting someone else down. I can't imagine any husband or wife putting up with it for long.

Even sadder are the instances in which parents bully their children by pointing out their flaws and mistakes to others in public. I've also seen parents order their children around in public with such cruelty that I can't imagine what life must be like at home for the poor kids. "Pull up your pants! Comb your hair! You look like a bum! Tie your shoelaces! Go do your homework, you lazy kid!" These are just some of the kinds of comments I've heard. Parenting like that scares me, because I can't imagine what those terribly bullied children will grow up to become. Seeing parents bully their children has made me even more determined to be a loving, yet firm, father and a husband who expresses his love by encouraging and building up those closest to him.

10. Resolve Problems and Misunderstandings When They Occur

Like many young married couples with a child, we have discovered that simply not talking about problems in the relationship or in our family life does not resolve anything. Buried issues have a tendency to rise again during arguments or when the flames of stress are running high.

Your tongue can do damage or it can heal. That is a choice we all have. A married couple who is learning to deal with their first child has to be especially sensitive to what they say and how they say it to each other. The additional stress of caring for a child and providing for a bigger family can have a double-edged effect. You are often weary and worn out, so you are less careful about what you say and less sensitive to the other person's feelings. On the other hand, you are also less able to gracefully receive what your spouse says to you and about you. Those two effects working together create a potentially volatile environment.

I'm sure I'm not the first husband and new father who wishes he had an Undo button for things he's said to his wife or children. One of my more unpleasant childhood memories is overhearing an argument between my parents when I was seven years old. At first, they weren't aware that I was within earshot because I was in the bathroom. I needed help getting out of there, but they'd gotten into an argument, and I waited and waited as their words became more and more heated. When I finally asked for help, it seemed they couldn't hear me.

I don't hold it against them. Even then I knew they were under tremendous stress. And besides, every married couple has to vent their frustration now and then. I'm sure this was a case when they wish they could have erased the whole thing from my memory.

They were still venting at each other when they realized I was in the bathroom waiting. My mum said, "Your son is ready to come out of the bathroom."

My father replied, "He is *your* son too!"

I know they didn't mean to, but their words hurt because I was already very sensitive about being a burden to my family. It was their heated moment and really had nothing to do with me. I understand that now, but I also understand how words exchanged in anger can cause long-term damage. I want to remember that as a father and husband. It's a lesson I want to apply to my life so that my children are never collateral damage in an argument with my wife.

Unfortunately, you can't erase things that have already been said, but you can apologize and air your feelings rather than let them fester. We all want to be loved and understood, and it is helpful to remember that, even when you are upset with your spouse. Instead of striking back or seeking revenge for a slight or perceived slight, I recommend resisting the urge to push your spouse away and instead draw closer by using healing and comforting words and touch.

Issues that go unresolved often surface again, and they become like a wedge in a log: every time you strike it, the split goes deeper and becomes more difficult to repair. Kanae and I try to resolve any conflicts before the end of the day. Following the directive to never go to bed angry does wonders for our sleep, not to mention our intimacy. It's really not fun lying in bed when one of you is spewing steam from the ears and nostrils. Talking it out is almost always a better idea than trying to ignore the rampaging elephant in the room. You don't have to come to complete agreement. You can even agree to disagree—or to talk it through the next day—as long as you do your best to understand your spouse's side of the issue.

Actually, one of the most empowering things I've learned to do is to give up the need to be right. I don't know about you, but at the end of the day, I'd much rather be snuggled than be right!

Fifteen

Heart and Home

*W*e were still on our honeymoon when my father called and left a message on my cell phone. He said there was a problem with the house we thought we were coming home to. We'd signed a contract to buy it before the wedding and planned on settling in as soon as we returned.

"Nick, I have bad news about your house, but don't worry, I found you another one," said Dad. "Trust me, it's perfect. But you have to move fast."

I could only roll my eyes in exasperation and think, *Uh, Dad, we're on our honeymoon!*

My father is a strong Christian, but he has secret passion. It's called real estate. I spent half my childhood riding around with him looking at houses that belonged to other people. Dad was more of a browser than a buyer. He still talks about real estate all the time. I think it's in his genes, because several of his relatives are in the real estate business in California. I've also inherited a bit of this bug, as I still love to look at houses. My dad also is something of a real estate psychic, or so he claimed when I called him from our Hawaii honeymoon spot. "I never felt peace about that other house, but I found a great one that's been in foreclosure and abandoned, and it is designed exactly for your needs," he said.

My needs for a home were that it be wheelchair accessible and Nick Vujicic affordable. This was my first house and our first house as a couple. I'd been working hard and saving money for a long time. The California real estate market, which would normally be way out of my reach, was in a recession. Suddenly, there were houses within my budget, but they were few and far between, and usually in foreclosure or short sales.

The house we'd put a contract on wasn't ideally designed for me, but we loved the views and the location. My dad had found problems with it during the inspection and decided to look for another house. Between you and me, I think my dad just loves to house shop, so I was a little concerned about his call. He must have picked up on that because the next thing I knew, he and Mum were sending me nearly three hundred photographs of the new house he'd found. He also asked if Kanae and I wanted our real estate agent cousins, Natalie and Lara, to do a virtual tour of the house via video.

I had to admit, the house and lot were impressive. The inside was a bit of a mess because the place had been empty for a while. It looked like some appliances were missing from the outdoor kitchen, but this was still an amazing house that sat on a beautiful piece of land with views for miles. The new house was single story with wide hallways that would easily accommodate my wheelchair. The icing on the cake was that it had a large pool with a waterfall and slide. Although it was only half finished, we saw potential. We love to swim, and the other house didn't have a pool.

My father thought we should submit an offer immediately. He faxed a contract to our hotel. Kanae and I were impressed with all the work Dad had put into his research. We felt comfortable enough to sign and fax it back to him. I said to my new wife, "Well, we just put an offer on a house without seeing it for ourselves."

Then I thought, *Never in a million years did I think I'd ever do that!*

Kanae smiled and gave me a squeeze, but I know she was thinking, *So this is what our marriage is going to be like...*

In truth, neither of us was too worried. I actually do trust my father's judgment on real estate matters, and we also had my real estate agents from Prime Realty, Uncle Batta's daughters, Natalie and Lara, on board. Besides, Kanae and I both knew that we would be happy together living in a shack. (And even happier if it had a pool!) We believe that Jesus has made His home in our hearts, and as long as we carry Him there, God's love will keep our love strong no matter where we are.

Before we married, Kanae and I had talked about wanting to make our home a peaceful and loving place, a sanctuary from my crazy, hectic life on the road. Our goal was to make our home and our marriage a refuge where our love for each other would grow deeper over the years.

That is important to our Creator too. In the Bible, we're told to greet everyone we meet with the words, "Peace be to you, peace to your house, and peace to all that you have!" The financial, emotional, and physical stress of modern life can take a toll on a relationship very quickly. Many marriages disintegrate because of outside pressures. We didn't want that to happen to us. We want our marriage and home to serve as our stronghold and refuge from the pressures of the world.

Home Is Where the Heart Is

When Kanae and I returned from our honeymoon, we were eager to see our new home. Dad and the agent kept us informed of all the work that went into securing the contract, and they'd put together a checklist of the work that needed to be done before we could move in.

The home had been custom built with many extra features, including a big outdoor patio with an outdoor kitchen and what appeared to have been a built-in grill, a fridge, and sinks. We couldn't tell with certainty what appliances the outdoor kitchen had featured because there were only holes where they had formerly been, and we knew we'd need some additional information in order to replace them with the correct models.

We had other questions about our new home too, so we looked up the name and phone number of the previous owner, though I wasn't sure about calling him. This had been a foreclosure, after all, and there can be strong emotions and feelings involved in losing a home.

I left a phone message saying we didn't want to bother them, but we had a few questions. I tried to be diplomatic, though I felt awkward because I had no idea what the whole story was. A few days later, the former owner called back. He was very gracious and helpful. He explained that he and his wife had built the house as their dream home with plans to live there many years, but then the recession hit and he lost his job. Their financial problems worsened when his wife, who'd had her own hair studio, sustained a back injury. She'd needed some surgery and there'd been complications, so she could no longer work. Then to top it all off, one of their contractors allegedly ran off with his payment but never finished the work he'd been hired to do. I felt very sad for them and for all of the problems they'd had.

"I'm sorry to have disturbed you," I said. "We will be good caretakers of this beautiful home, and we will honor all the love you put into it. It's a dream for us to have such a wonderful place to live."

He thanked me, and I asked if I could pray for him and his family, explaining that I am a Christian evangelist and an inspirational speaker. Then he told me something quite moving.

"Nick, I know exactly who you are, and we would love to have you pray for us," he said. "When all these problems occurred four years ago, we were heavy-hearted and depressed about leaving this home. My family cried together, but we also prayed and thanked God for our family, our friends, and all who had helped us and comforted us in our time of need."

He went on to say that in the most difficult moments of their grief and sorrow, he'd gone on the Internet looking for solace and inspiration, and he'd come across my videos. At the time, of course, they had no idea Kanae and I would someday seek to buy their house.

"We watched the videos as a family, and we all cried because you were showing us how our faith in God could get us through this just as yours had led you to your purpose and a wonderful life," the previous owner said.

He didn't discover that we were the buyers of his former home until all of the paperwork was done and he checked public records. He told me, "We gathered the family, and I told them they would never believe who bought our house—the young guy with no limbs who had provided us all with such inspiration on the YouTube videos. He is now living in our home, and I can't think of a better person to have it."

What I had feared would be an awkward and perhaps painful exchange with the former owner turned out to be something quite wonderful. God had to bring us all together for a reason, and part of it may have been a lesson for my wife and me. The previous owners built a house out of love and commitment to each other and their children. Then a terrible series of events beyond their control forced them to give up their home. They grieved the loss, as anyone would, but they realized also that they still had each other, and the love in God that bonded them together saw them through this tragedy.

THE THREE CORDS THAT BIND

When I spoke with the previous owner on the phone, I was struck by the positive tone in his voice. Despite all that they had been through and the losses they had suffered, he sounded like a man at peace with the world. After hearing this family's story, I know that the strength of their faith in God and their love for each other inspired Kanae and me. Their story reminded us that it doesn't matter how nice your home is. You could lose the house and all of your earthly possessions in a very short period. What truly matters is the strength of your faith and the loving bonds you share with those who matter most to you.

The Bible tells us that a person standing alone can easily be attacked and defeated, but two—as in a married couple—can stand back-to-back and conquer. Yet three is even better. If God is part of your lives and the lives of your loved ones, then you have a triple-braided cord that is not easily broken at all. You can have a house built of the strongest materials available, but faith and family are your only true shelter and refuge from misfortune, hardship, and the cruelty of the world.

Your true home on earth, then, is in the heart. It is a place where you aren't judged or condemned or pressured by the expectations of others. I mentioned earlier that I found such relief as a boy when I'd come home after being bullied, teased, or shunned by classmates in school. Home was the place where I always fit in, where I didn't have to watch everything I did or worry about being stared at or made fun of because I was different.

Now I have my home with Kanae and Kiyoshi, and it's even better. As our love grows and our marriage moves into new seasons, we want to keep working on strengthening our bonds. We can do that in our beautiful home, but we can also nurture our love anywhere and everywhere we go.

Kanae and I don't ever want to lose sight of the fact that our priorities are first God, next each other, and finally our family. God gives us the foundation for everything else, which is why faith must be first and foremost. If it weren't for God's plan, Kanae and I would not be together, nor would we be blessed with our son.

In Service to Each Other

Kanae told me recently that our house, as much as she loves it, is not a home until I'm there too, and I feel the same about her and Kiyoshi. The challenge we all face, or at least the challenge we all need to recognize and take on, is not to build bigger and bigger homes. The only important challenge is to build stronger and stronger bonds with our spouse, children, and our other loved ones. With God's help, we will create an environment that only brings us closer in our faith and in our love for each other.

There is an aspect to our relationship that is different from many marriages, though not all, of course. In addition to the usual work and responsibilities of being a wife and mother, Kanae has to help me deal with the challenges of having no arms and no legs. I wish it were not that way, but we have decided not to have a live-in caregiver, at least for now.

This means extra work and responsibility for Kanae, and I am always aware of that. My friend and mentor Joni Eareckson Tada has written a great deal about the many challenges her husband, Ken, has overcome while serving as both her spouse and caregiver.

Joni requires more assistance than I normally do because I'm more mobile, but even so, Kanae has to do many things for me. Think about the hundreds of daily tasks that require the use of limbs, whether it's preparing and eating a meal, tidying up the house, bathing, or even scratching the top of your head. I've figured out the ways to do maybe two-thirds of those tasks without limbs so that I do not require assistance. Yet there are still certain things that I simply cannot do on my own without great difficulty, some ingenious contraptions, or risking injury to my neck, which already gets abused more than most necks.

Kanae amazes me every day in the way she helps me with such grace. She often tells people that she hardly thinks about the fact that I have no limbs. I might have difficulty believing that if she didn't live that way each and every day. She helps me instinctively and without resentment.

It's also true that because of my disabilities, I can't help her as much as most husbands help their wives. Most can lend a hand with the baby when his wife has other duties or is worn out, but there's not a lot I can do other than try to keep Kiyoshi occupied and happy. He loves chasing me around the house and riding on my wheelchair with me. I enjoy entertaining him, of course. It would be even better if I could change his diaper, bathe him, put him in bed when he is tired, and take him out when he awakens.

There is no doubt that Kanae has more of a daily workload than most wives, but she handles it with such patience that my love for her grows each day. I've tried to find ways to ask for her assistance without being demanding or adding to her stress load. I don't always succeed, but I'm determined to be as low maintenance as I can, while helping her, serving her, and showing my love for her in every way possible.

A Marriage Built on Faith and Small, Daily Kindnesses

Jesus provided the ultimate example for unselfishness when He gave His life for our sins by dying on the cross. There is no greater love than that. When we have a personal relationship with Jesus, we give up our own desires and needs and give our life to Him. When we marry someone, the same model applies. We give up the selfish one to become a selfless two. Our marriage and our family take precedence over our individual needs and desires.

How does having a servant's heart work in a marriage? For starters, it will not work, nor will the marriage, if you expect your spouse to serve you. It will work if you live to serve your spouse. I know that sounds incredibly idealistic or naive or impossible to accomplish day in and day out. Yet in the best marriages I've seen, that is exactly how the husbands and wives treat each other, and they seem to do it instinctively. I'm not saying they do it every minute every day, but they seem to have made it a way of life.

My longtime role models for a great marriage are Victor and Elsie Schlatter, who have been married nearly sixty years. They are American friends of my family who work as missionaries at South Pacific Island Ministries, based in Australia. The Schlatters, who are now in their eighties, ministered to the people of Papua New Guinea for decades. Victor is an author, and he translated the Bible into the native languages of the people of New Guinea.

I've known the Schlatters since I was about six years old. I went to their church camp, where they treated me so warmly—and I say that quite literally, since Victor would have me help him start the campfires we needed to fend off the cold. My first year at their camp, the heel of my little foot split open from the cold, dry weather, and Elsie saw that it was hurting me. I told a little fib, saying I'd split it while skateboarding, and I always felt guilty about that since she was so nice to me. (True confession, Elsie!) She bandaged it and gave me lotion, so I think she knew it was just dryness, but she pretended to believe me and prayed with me.

Elsie and Victor became my vision of living saints. Over the years, we stayed close. They were big encouragers for me. When many people expressed serious doubts about my ability to undertake a worldwide ministry, Victor and Elsie blessed me with their support and prayed for my success.

They have blessed Kanae and me with their example as a married couple whose love for each other has no limits. They travel around the world together, and I've sometimes met up with them on their trips. They are always praising each other, laughing and smiling, and they appear to always strive to make each other feel loved.

No Gimmicks, Just Giving

Describing Victor and Elsie's marriage is difficult. I want to say that they really work at serving and loving each other, but really what they do seems effortless because there is so much genuine affection between them. I asked Uncle Vic how they have kept their bond so strong over the years, and he said, "It's not a gimmick or a tactic. It is our relationship with the Father and our three-braided cord, which is not easily broken."

Victor was in his third year at Purdue University in the United States, studying to be a nuclear engineer and preparing for a career with General Electric (GE), when he met Elsie. She had a strong Christian upbringing. "I was not really that much molded into the same outlook, but I believed there was a God and I had a relationship with Him," Victor recalled. "Mostly, I was looking for the good life when I met her. I liked fishing and other fun things."

On their first date, Elsie told Victor that she wanted to spend her life following the gospel. He was studying engineering, and her desire seemed like a waste of time to him.

Victor liked Elsie, but the rest of the date didn't go very well. That night after going to bed, Victor had a change of heart. He prayed for God's guidance, saying, "Lord, if You need this young lady to help me be where You want me to be, here I am."

He likes to joke that he was a shallow man until Elsie came around, but after meeting her, Victor realized that Elsie had something that he needed in his life. "She was really good looking, but there are a lot of good-looking people," he said. "She had more than that; she had a spirit that I needed. I had a background in mathematics and science, but I needed God to be in the equation, otherwise my life would be just second rate."

Victor graduated early from college and worked for GE's nuclear engineering department for seven years before he decided that the God part of the equation was the most important part for him and his wife to focus upon. They began their missionary life then and have continued ever since.

"We have had a very, very blessed life," he told me.

One of the most impressive features of their marriage is that they have deeply engrained habits that are all built around expressing their love and appreciation for each other. For example, every Friday, Elsie reads Proverbs 31 to Victor. This is the proverb that talks about the virtuous wife, saying, "Who can find a virtuous wife? For her worth is far above rubies. The heart of her husband safely trusts her.... She does him good and not evil all the days of her life."

I'd say Elsie has done Victor quite a bit of good over the many years of their marriage. She shared with me a short appreciation note she wrote about Victor. She won first prize for it in a contest for spouses of ministers.

I am privileged to share my life with the most unique husband in the world. Accepting responsibility early because of his father's premature death, Victor swept floors in a shop for a few cents! Later he dug graves with a shovel for a few dollars! Later he was employed as a nuclear chemist in the US for large sums! Then at God's call, he dropped everything for Bible translation in Papua New Guinea. Now he is an author and speaker! During our engagement, I told him I needed a husband that would tell me daily, "I love you!" For sixty-one years, he has never missed a day! He is truly a Psalm 1 man!

I've traveled with Victor and Elsie and spent many days and nights with them, and their unity and love for each other always amazes me. They praise each other constantly, and they always seem to be focused on serving each other's needs.

HUMBLE SERVICE

The Bible describes the servant leader role as one in which you "let nothing be done through selfish ambition or conceit, but in lowliness of mind let each esteem others better than himself. Let each of you look out not only for his own interests, but also for the interests of others."

It's not about the husband or wife being superior or acting superior to each other. The emphasis isn't on being a servant. It's on serving, as in being there for each other, anticipating needs, helping, and putting each other first without jealousy or competition or any of those other feelings that can derail a marriage.

How does the concept of serving your spouse in a marriage work in real life? Is it possible to always put your spouse's interest, desires, and happiness ahead of your own? I have friends who laugh at the thought of that. Another friend said it's easy for him because his wife keeps this slogan on the refrigerator: "If mama ain't happy, ain't nobody happy!"

Seriously, I might be tempted to believe that a marriage like that has never existed, except that I've observed Elsie and Victor all of these years, and they truly live to serve each other. I think the secret is that, as Victor noted, they don't make a big show of it, but they live it by finding small ways to express love and kindness throughout each day. They anticipate each other's needs. They help out. They say sweet things, hug, and touch.

I'm sure they must get exasperated and frustrated sometimes, but honestly, I've never heard them exchange cross words. They just have this attitude that drives their behavior, and their attitude is that each considers the other a blessing.

One of the concerns I hear from other men when I talk about serving their wife first is, "What if I serve her first all the time, but she doesn't do the same for me?" That seems to be a big issue for many people. *What if I give up everything and get nothing in return?*

The answer to this lies in your faith and the strength of it. My own answer to this is that I want to serve Kanae not because I want to get something in return but because I believe I am honoring God when I put her first and foremost in my life. As long as God is at the center of my life, I don't expect anything in return from Kanae.

My rewards will come, not just in having a great marriage, but also in heaven. We want to inspire others with our lasting love for each other. We want our marriage to be like a city on a hill that brings light to those around us.

By putting the person you love first in your life and in your actions, you are showing your love and honoring your marriage vows. If your spouse doesn't live the same way by putting you first, then you may need to talk about why that is so and what can be done about it. Sometimes a husband and wife need to go back and call to mind what it was that brought them together.

As a final offering in this book, Kanae and I have some suggestions for things you and your spouse can do to keep the bonds of love and marriage strong. We hope these will help you continue to grow closer, just as we want to be like Victor and Elsie—still very much in love after more than sixty years together. They serve as proof that we all can do that if we are willing to put each other first to glorify not ourselves but God who brought us together.

Daily Steps to Strengthen Your Bond

Start the Day Together

We mentioned earlier that we have made it a habit to read the Bible together for a half hour to an hour when we awaken. We've derived more benefit from this than you can imagine. It gives us such a peaceful feeling and sets us off on our days as a couple confident in our unified strength. As Christians, we find it helpful and inspiring to start the morning this way, but any activity that brings you closer will work. You might find it better to go for a walk, listen to music, or just have coffee and breakfast together to quietly discuss your plans, dreams, and the state of your relationship.

Keep the Romance Alive

Having a baby in the house has definitely brought changes to our love life. Every couple I know tells pretty much the same story. Privacy and spontaneity go out the window with a little one, but that doesn't mean you can't make adjustments and improvise. If you're a husband, please keep in mind that women generally have to be emotionally engaged, so if you've been caught up in work, unable to communicate with her, or absent for several days, you need to be intentional about reconnecting with her emotionally before you make an effort to reconnect physically.

Back rubs, hugs, focused conversations, and attentiveness to each other are all small things that can help you fire up the romantic connections. (In my case, this sometimes requires a little creativity. Yes, I've been known to massage Kanae's back with my chin!)

Remember that buying her flowers, chocolates, a romantic dinner, or a sexy nightgown will only work if you've helped her feel loved and connected to you before the gift arrives. Staying connected isn't something you do in your spare time. It's something you do at every opportunity. When I watch Elsie and Victor, I'm amazed that they still seem to be very physically engaged with each other. They are constantly hugging, touching, cuddling, and involved in intimate conversations, and given the longevity of their marriage, they must be doing something right.

Date Nights

I confess that when I was a single guy, I thought date nights for married couples seemed a little sad and a bit contrived. "You have to set up a date with your wife? Dude, what if she tells you she has other plans?" Now, of course, I get it.

Life as a parent is so hectic that you need to set a specific time to reconnect as a couple. This is why knowing a reliable baby-sitter is suddenly more important than having a good auto mechanic.

I know married couples who are very committed to date nights, and their children understand that Mommy and Daddy always seem to enjoy getting away together.

Kanae and I have joined the date night trend. The challenge is to leave all of our work and baby thoughts behind and just focus on each other and our feelings. One rule: don't talk about money or job stress. I know a guy who took his wife out for an intimate Valentine's Day dinner and then ruined it by announcing that he'd accepted a job in another town and they'd have to uproot the family. Talk about killing the romance!

Mini Trips or Vacations

This one is a challenge if you don't have family members who you trust to watch your child, but there are many benefits to getting away, even if just for a night or two. Anniversaries are a good time to do this, of course. When your children are young, you may just find a place a few miles away. When they are teenagers, maybe you should just pitch a tent in the backyard or sleep in the garage. *Kidding!* I have older married friends who established this tradition early on, and it has become a big event for them now that their children are grown and out of the house. They may not take an anniversary trip every year, but they save up and take one every few years to enjoy each other and to celebrate their lives together.

Be a Friend with Benefits

Frankly, I think this whole concept works best for married couples, even though its origins, as I understand it, were in the singles world. Study after study has shown that most of the successful marriages are those in which the man and woman spent time as friends before becoming lovers. I'm not sure how you can become lovers without being friends first, but then again, I've led a fairly sheltered life. You do actually have to like the person you are married to, right?

So buddy up! By that I mean find activities that you both enjoy and do them. This can be a hobby like antique hunting or fishing (my favorite!); a physical activity like boating, hiking, bicycling, or rock climbing; or more relaxed like going to movies, cooking meals, or hitting the beach.

Kanae and I went skydiving together before Kiyoshi was born, but I don't think we'll be doing that again. Our desire to take risks together has diminished considerably, but we do enjoy boating, swimming, surfing, and fishing together. Sharing favorite activities helps us reconnect as friends and reminds us that our son is just one of many interests we have in common—even if he is number one.

Go Out with Other Couples Who Really Like Each Other

This may be more difficult than it sounds, because so many husbands and wives tend to snipe, bicker, badger, and take shots at each other when they are out with other couples. Even couples who get along well with each other when they are alone do this as a twisted form of entertainment when out with friends. They may enjoy it, but it defeats the purpose, which is to bring you and your wife closer together. I find that being with couples who truly love each other— like Elsie and Victor—is inspiring to Kanae and me. We learn from them about how to be closer, and we see that love and friendship can endure over the long term. It may take you a while to find a couple who can have fun without throwing darts at each other, but when you do, they can help your relationship through their example. (And you can help them!)

Live, Love, and Laugh

Kanae gave me a wake-up call recently when she said, "We laughed all the time before we were married. I miss that."

Ouch! As much as it pained me to admit it, my wife was right. Some of my fondest memories of our courtship were the many times we were overcome with laughter to the point that neither of us could breathe.

What happened?

My knee-jerk response is that we just got caught up in the urgency of life, preparing for Kiyoshi's arrival, adjusting to his presence in our life, and settling into being a family of three. But really, there is no excuse for living and loving without laughter. One of my greatest weapons against bullies, depression, and isolation has been my sense of humor. There were so many times when I disarmed a potential bully by cracking a joke about my disability, or the bully's inability to deal with my disability.

Even though I make my living speaking on serious issues, humor has always been a part of my presentations. I learned early on that people quickly get over my unique appearance when I make them laugh at themselves or me or each other. Humor has healing power, and we all need it in our marriage. It's the cheapest form of therapy I can imagine.

One couple I know has been married nearly thirty years, and they still find ways to make each other laugh each and every day. For one of his birthdays, the wife presented her husband, who is not a skilled repairman, a gag rubber hand in a toolbox. She included a note saying that she knew he often "needed a hand" with his chores around the house.

He responded by hiding the hand in one of her blouses so that it dropped out when she went to put it on. That set off "hand wars" that have been going on for several years now. It's not sophisticated, but it makes them laugh, and in a sense, it is another way of serving each other's needs and staying engaged with each other.

Kanae and I have running jokes about what she can do to me if I ever misbehave or make her angry. So far the options she has mentioned include using our son's baby fence to prevent me from leaving my home office, or putting me in our very deep bathtub or Kiyoshi's crib, which I can't escape without help. I'm just hoping she never realizes that I could fit into our freezer.

Maybe you and your wife aren't pranksters or practical jokers, but even watching television comedies, funny movies, or YouTube videos can bring more laughter into your life.

Love Without Limits

One of our greatest sources for bonding and fulfillment is our son, of course. Kiyoshi has brought so much depth and delight to our marriage. As a single guy, I had never imagined how much I could love my child. Nor had I expected that what I would love most about him is that we share this same deep love for his mother. I could spend every day watching my son and wife interact. Kanae takes such joy in his hugs and laughter, and Kiyoshi obviously adores her, just as I do.

I missed our son's first successful effort to stand when I was away on tour, but I was there for his first steps. When I was gone, I would speak to Kiyoshi on the telephone or on Skype, and I'd tell him not to speak any words, get any teeth, or take any steps until I could return. Fortunately, he held out.

We were on a trip together in Hawaii when he took his first solo flight. I had a series of speaking engagements all over the islands, so we were hopping around for four weeks from place to place. As it happened, we were staying in Maui, at the same hotel where Kanae and I had honeymooned about two years earlier, when our son decided he'd had enough of crawling.

I had looked forward to this day for several reasons. I had been able to hold Kiyoshi in the baby sling for only a brief few weeks during his infancy, because he quickly gained weight beyond what my tender spine could bear. And, from his earliest days, Kiyoshi has never reached out for me to pick him up even though he has always done this with Kanae and his grandmothers, aunts, and uncles.

Apparently, he recognized early on that his father has no arms, so instead, he just hugs me or gives me a high-five slap on my shoulder. I find this beyond heartwarming. It is as joyous an experience as anything I've ever felt. Yet I had been wondering what would happen when Kiyoshi started walking. You know how babies are when they first start to walk. Sometimes they get up and their momentum carries them forward a few quick steps, and then they crash and burn unless someone is there to catch them. I pondered whether he would be hesitant to come to me, knowing it was more of a risk since I had no hands to catch him if he fell.

I imagined that coming to me would seem to him like walking a tightrope without a safety net: my son, the Flying Wallenda! You can imagine my wonder and joy when on his first series of staggering strolls across our hotel room carpet, Kiyoshi looked intently into my eyes, tucked his chin with determination, and made his way toward me.

Oh, my gosh, it was so beautiful to see his courage as he came haltingly across the room toward his daddy, who had no hands to catch and hold him. He was smiling with delight at every faltering step, chugging along with no fear until he reached me—and then something magical happened, or so it seemed to me.

My son didn't pause for me to pick him up; instead, his chubby little hands grabbed hold of my shirt, my collarbone, my shoulders, wherever he could get a good grip. Then he pulled close and landed against me, docking there safely, beaming delightfully, and feeling so proud of himself!

I nearly lost it. I flashed back to all the days of my life I'd spent fretting over whether I would ever find a woman, get married, and have a family. *Who would want me? Who would love me? Who would want to have children with me? Is there love available for a man such as me?*

The answer, as displayed in Kiyoshi's mad dash to his daddy, is *Yes!*

And the answer is *Yes!* for you too. We are all God's children. We are all worthy of love. If you have it in your heart to be married and have a family one day, please take our story as validation of those dreams. And please remember the important messages of this book:

- Never give up on love if love is what you want, because God planted that desire in your heart for a purpose.
- You are worthy of love because you are the creation of a loving Father.
- There is someone out there who could love you and share your life.
- A successful marriage requires reciprocal and unselfish love, as well as a shared, deep, and lasting commitment.
- Parenthood will test your marriage. It will also strengthen your bonds of love, but only if you develop deep empathy and unwavering support for each other by putting your family's welfare above self-interest.
- The "work" of being married is mostly about giving up our naturally self-centered ways and learning day by day to put God first, our spouse and family second, and ourselves third.
- Your marriage, your family, and your home should always be a safe, loving, caring, and comforting place—a refuge from the world and all of its challenges.

Most of all, I hope you will embrace the existence of love without limits. You may feel that everything else in the world has its limitations. I know my wisdom is limited, as is my physical strength. We all are limited in many ways, but we all can choose to love without limits according to the power of Jesus Christ, who transforms me on a daily basis. He makes me a better husband. He makes me a better father. He makes me a better child of God.

Have faith that you will find the love you seek, and know that you have the capacity to love without limits just as Jesus Christ showed His love for us. God will help you love your spouse and children first of all, and they will teach you more about love without limits than you thought you could ever know.

Kanae and Kiyoshi make me want to be a better man and a better Christian every day. I want to prove myself worthy of their limitless love, and I want to drink up as much of it as I can on this earth.

I am so thankful that Kanae joined me in writing this book, because now you know her and the depth of her love as I have experienced it. She is my role model for someone who has tapped into its transformative powers for healing wounds and giving strength. Of all the people I've known, she is the most inspiring because of the way she loves me, an imperfect man in so many ways. Her love is patient. It is kind. It is merciful, tolerant, and encouraging. Her love always protects, always trusts, always hopes, and always perseveres.

God has blessed me beyond measure with His love and that of this beautiful woman and the child we share. We pray for you and with you that if you haven't already found love, one day soon you, too, will be able to bask in love without limits.

We love you.

—Nick, Kanae, and Kiyoshi

ACKNOWLEDGMENTS

All thanks and glory to God—the Father, Son, and Holy Spirit. To our immediate families, relatives, and friends, thank you for your unconditional love, prayers, and support for our family and ministry. We love you all very much. Thanks to our writing partner, Wes Smith, for doing another amazing written work of inspiration to help change lives for the better. Thank you to my literary agents—Jan Miller, Nena Madonia, and the team at Dupree Miller and Associates—for believing in this ministry. Thanks to the Crown Publishing Group. And thanks to the WaterBrook Multnomah Publishing Group—president and CEO Steve Cobb, senior editor Bruce Nygren, and senior production editor Laura Wright.

I would like to acknowledge David Price, his wife, Helen, their families, and Oaks Christian School for all the years of faith-filled love and generous support toward the Life Without Limbs ministry. David, we thank you for propelling us forward, onward, and upward for the glory of God as a brother in Christ and board member. A very special thank you to the board of directors, the advisory board, and the entire staff and team of Life Without Limbs for all of your prayers, hard work, and passion to see Jesus proclaimed in all the earth.

Thank you to the staff and team of Attitude Is Altitude for dreaming with me on how to be creative in packaging messages of inspiration and love, leading to messages of faith and true hope.

Lastly, it is our joy to give a heartfelt thanks to all who have been following and supporting the Life Without Limbs mission as a volunteer, financial partner, and prayer warrior for the ministry. We all truly thank God for each and every one of you. Please keep in your prayers and heart the ministry and our blessed family.

Kiyoshi—Mummy and Daddy love you very, very much. Forgive us and be patient with us as we continue to be better parents by God's grace each day. We love you.

Babe, love you.

Love you too, babe.

About the Author

Nick Vujicic is an evangelist, motivational speaker, and the director of Life Without Limbs, an organization that preaches the gospel of Jesus Christ and helps alleviate the suffering of mankind.

Born without limbs, Nick has become a great inspirational voice to people all around the world, totaling so far fifty-four countries and more than three thousand speaking engagements. He regularly speaks to large crowds in stadiums, meets with presidents and other government officials, and addresses educational coalitions, business leaders, students, and the poor and needy. He speaks on overcoming obstacles, never giving up, and how to find purpose, faith, and hope.

A frequent subject of media coverage, Nick has been interviewed by *CBS Sunday Morning*, *Oprah's LifeClass*, ABC TV's *20/20*, the *Los Angeles Times*, TBN, the *700 Club*, James and Betty Robisons' *Life Today*, *Joni and Friends*, Janet Parshall, Joel Osteen, Dr. James Dobson's *Family Talk*, and others in the Unites States. Abroad, he's been featured twice on *60 Minutes Australia*, and in 2013 he was on live television in twelve countries as a keynote speaker to four hundred million viewers.

A longtime resident of Australia, he now lives in Southern California with his wife and coauthor of this book, Kanae, and their son, Kiyoshi.

Find out more by visiting www.lifewithoutlimbs.org
and www.attitudeisaltitude.com.

NO BULLY CAN DEFINE
WHO YOU ARE

Born without arms or legs, Nick Vujicic knows what it's like to be different. And he knows what it's like to be bullied—and rise above it. In *Stand Strong*, Nick gives you strategies for responding to the bullies in your life, empowering you to feel more confident than you ever felt before.

Read a chapter excerpt on www.WaterBrookMultnomah.com!

Being unstoppable is about believing and achieving.
It's about having faith in yourself, your talents, your
purpose, and most of all, in God's great love
and His divine plan for your life.

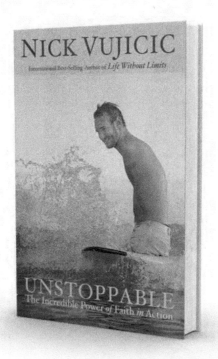

Motivational speaker Nick Vujicic details his own battles with despair
and provides tangible advice for anyone who feels overwhelmed with
the burdens of life.

Read a chapter excerpt on www.WaterBrookMultnomah.com!

What Would Your Life be Like if *Anything* Were Possible?

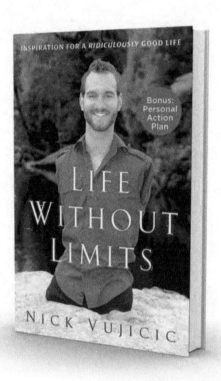

Nick Vujicic shares how his faith in God has been his major source of strength, and he explains that once he found a sense of purpose—inspiring others to better their lives and the world around them—he found the confidence to build a rewarding and productive life without limits. Let Nick inspire you to start living your own life without limits.

Read a chapter excerpt on www.WaterBrookMultnomah.com!